DATE DUE			
APR 18 '83			
MAY 8 '89			
MAY 2 5 1994			

THE BROADER WAY

THE
BROADER WAY

A Woman's Life in the New Japan

SUMIE SEO MISHIMA

GREENWOOD PRESS, PUBLISHERS
WESTPORT, CONNECTICUT

CONTENTS

THE BROADER WAY

Part One

THE WAR YEARS

~~~~~~

1. Retrospect

The war that ended in the moral and economic bankruptcy of the Japanese people, and that has brought problems of increased gravity and complexity for the world to face and, if possible, solve, has most strangely and unexpectedly brought me that final deliverance for which I have struggled so patiently and so desperately since 1928.

I was educated in America. The five years in the middle 1920s that I spent in the United States as a young student were the most decisive years in my life. Warmly received into the midst of American prosperity, great liberalism and international goodwill, I took in as much as I possibly could of the best of American culture. Feeling myself a transformed human being and an accomplished citizen of the world, I came home, via Europe and the Orient to my native land of Japan. I thought I was now an "emancipated" woman, freed from the bondage of feudalistic customs which still lay heavily on Japanese women, and from the revolt which had been the chief motive for my going to America. I thought I could now work for the modernization of the Japanese people.

I had been deceived, however. In Tokyo all I could find to do was some tutoring and part-time teaching in elementary English. Japan was then at the bottom of a terrible economic depression, and no one was interested in American liberalism. It was out of the question that I should ever get a job where I could use my precious foreign experience, or one which would repay me even in the least proportion for the enormous sum of money expended on my studies abroad.

I now turned to the study of Far Eastern history—history was the subject I got most interested in while in the United States—and was admitted as one of the few women among six thousand men students in a Tokyo university. Japanese universities, with only a few exceptions, were still closed to women at this time, and since these few had rigid academic qualifications for women applicants, I had to content myself with being a mere listener.

At the university I came to know a professor of China's economic history. His grandfather, a scholar in Chinese classics and teacher to the Emperor Taisho, was one of the most honored figures of the Meiji-Taisho period. I called on him at his home, and knew his mother and children. I was told that his wife, a beautiful woman whom I saw at his house only once, was working outside the home. I was not surprised to find his family living in this condition because I knew that his father had squandered the fortune and family honor bequeathed by his illustrious grandfather, and had died some years before, leaving the family in straitened circumstances.

One day the professor told me that his wife had left him and the children for good. Some time later he asked me to marry him. I had been fascinated by his lectures at the university, and I now thought I could be happily married to him. But I could not imagine myself suddenly mothering four little children. His mother, charming, sociable, obliging and energetic, and still vigorous in her fifties, seemed to encourage me. She said she would take care of the children so that I could continue studying and teaching. So finally, making light of the anxious disapproval of all my relatives and friends, I was married in the spring of 1932. I knew my road would not be easy, but I still had confidence in my American education.

I had an idea then that my marriage was to be entirely a personal affair between my husband and myself, in which my mother-in-law and my husband's children would be coordinated. But the moment I was married I saw my mistake. I had married into a matriarchy, solidly entrenched in the ancient social traditions of the Japanese people, where my costly American college education was totally useless. The web of contemporary Japanese life, with its conflict between the old and new, had caught me unaware.

I refused to be defeated. I naturally thought of divorce, but I did not like to face the "didn't we tell you so?" of my relatives and friends. My husband entreated me to stay, and I did not exactly want to go back to the status of an unmarried woman. True, I would then have plenty of time for reading and research to suit my tastes, but I feared I would be shut out mentally and emotionally from the reality of Japanese life. When, moreover, I learned the history of my husband's family, packed to the brim with the feudal ideal of family honor, I came to understand my mother-in-law's matriarchal claims. I understood the essence of the Japanese feudal system and its stand with regard to the influx of modern world civilization into the country.

I could not, however, meet my mother-in-law's demands. What I could do was to earn money by teaching and tutoring, and hire a maid who would do the housework which was properly required of me as daughter-in-law of the family. The august lady consented, though grudgingly, to this arrangement because, faced with the fact that my husband's teaching salaries were not large enough to support the family, my earnings became warmly welcome. The price of my freedom from the grip of domestic slavery was expensive, because I had to hire a place of my own where, freed from family complications, I could collect as many pupils as possible for tutoring and class work. I had to earn much more money than did my husband.

My financial responsibility grew still heavier when my mother-in-law took the four children, because of their delicate health, to Kamakura, a fashionable seaside town not far from Tokyo, and decided to live there with them and a maid, while my husband and I worked in Tokyo. Now I labored from early morning until late at night every day including Saturdays and Sundays. But the harder I worked the higher obstacles arose in my way. A working woman in Japan had to fight not only family sentiments, but also the prejudices of the general public. She had to accept stoically the wide wage discrimination against her sex, patiently handle the Japanese show of gentility about money matters, and smilingly put up with the bias of her husband's friends against a working wife. In addition, at that time I had to take into grave account the fact of the business depression, and of the fascist ascendency in the country which was driving working women back into their homes.

Against all these odds I struggled as hard as I could, but at last I had to admit that I was ruining my health. I now experimented on writing in English, and with the help of my American friends here and in the United States, I began to write for American readers.

The publication of my first book, *My Narrow Isle,** brought a ray of hope into my life. But this was early in 1941, and already the Japanese army was overrunning the continent of China, and the international situation was becoming more intense. Several months later, economic relations between the United States and Japan were disrupted.

And in December of that year, came Pearl Harbor. I was swept away with the rest of the world into the horrors and hellish sufferings of war. My deliverance was not to come until the terror had run its course.

* The John Day Company, 1941.

2. A Housewife's Struggles

From the beginning of the China War in 1937 straight through to the end of the Pacific War I kept saying over and over again to myself, "When will they stop fighting?" For more than eight years it was the only sincere thought in my mind and heart. The rest of my thoughts and my conduct were just mechanical responses to a powerful, irresistible set of outward circumstances.

As a Buddhist-Christian, I was opposed to war of any kind. But it was only within my family circle and among my friends that I could openly and unhesitatingly denounce our militarists' aggressions.

I well remember the day in the early stages of the China War when a high-school classmate and I shuddered together at the news of Japanese planes indiscriminately bombing the city of Shanghai. "We'll have to pay for this some day," my friend said. And quite unusually, in her soft, dark eyes I saw a flame of indignation and terrible presentiment deeply burning. "Yes, we'll have to pay for this," I echoed. But neither she nor I knew then what tribulations the Japanese people were fated to undergo as payment for their blind following after unwise leadership.

As far as my family and friends were concerned, they were all against war. I still wonder why these peaceful-minded Japanese—who must have formed a considerable portion of the population—could not have prevented the development of that awful tragedy.

But I did not have much time to think or talk about war. I had four fast-growing step-children to feed, clothe and send to school in face of the ever aggravated living conditions. They had all finished primary school in Kamakura, and the oldest one had also finished high school before she came up to live under our care in Tokyo. When the youngest child joined us, their grandmother came, too. Since our house was too small for such a large family, we rented another small one in the neighborhood for the grandmother's use, and the four children shuffled around between the two households. The expense of maintaining two houses and paying for the children's high school and college educations was frightful. Also their clothes had to be renewed constantly to keep up with their rapid growth, and this at a time when cotton and wool were fast disappearing from the market.

The older girl, Kazuko, after finishing high school, entered the Tokyo Women's Christian College. Soon, however, I realized that this most liberal of women's colleges in Japan was only suitable for rich girls who could devote their time completely to their intellectual and moral development without being bothered by the thought of earning a living. The tradition of the College had been to educate women to develop their personalities fully so that their beautiful Christian spirit of service and self-sacrifice would be appreciated under whatever economic and social conditions they might face in the future. But *my* conviction was that in a country like Japan, where women

—and particularly college women—had so few economic opportunities worthy of their education, a technical background was necessary before they could hope to have any practical influence on the people around them.

So with the backing of a cousin of my husband's, a progressively minded medical student, I advised Kazuko to take a medical course. She was a girl with a strong sense of duty who was readily influenced by other people's moral and intellectual wisdom, so she said she would try—that since many girls were studying medicine, she saw no reason why she could not do it. She passed the entrance examinations to the Tokyo Women's Medical College. It was the oldest medical institution for Japanese women, founded by a Japanese woman doctor, and renowned for its able graduates, who included not only Japanese women but also women of some other Far Eastern countries. Our friends were surprised to learn that such a sweet-tempered, delicate looking girl was studying to become a doctor. Her grandmother was horrified at first, but got over the shock shortly. The old lady had become far more yielding than she used to be.

The two boys went to the same high school, an expensive private school with a liberal minded principal, where my husband taught Oriental history. The older boy speeded through the seven grades with high marks, although hampered at one time by ill health, and advanced to the law department of the Tokyo Imperial University. The younger boy could not keep up with the high academic standards, and had to be transferred to another school.

My youngest step-daughter, Yasuko, a sweet-faced, sensitive child, was put in the high school founded and headed by Miss Kawai, a famous Christian educator.

And then came the biggest shock of my life—the news of Pearl Harbor. My husband was turning the radio dial early that morning, and quite unexpectedly caught the announcement. "They've done it!" he shouted. I jumped up and shuddered all over. I felt as if the catastrophe of heaven and earth, with all the fires of vengeance—the bombs—was about to rain on the Japanese people. I had not yet seen a bomb dropped, but had been told about their devastating horror. All that day I was startled by the slightest noise. The next morning when I awoke to a peaceful day with everything in the house and in the neighborhood unchanged from the previous day, I felt very strange. Apparently the war was still far off.

During the next few years I was to forget that I had had an American education, and that I had friends in the United States. All day and every day, when not called to an air-raid drill, or to community labor service for building an emergency waterpool, or to overhaul an evacuated house, I was to labor for food for the family.

Somehow it never occurred to me to ask whether Japan would win or lose. I could not associate such sporting terms as winning and losing with the terrible tragedy of a world war. I could only say, more and more desperately, "When will they stop fighting?"

3. The Neighborhood Society

About a year before Pearl Harbor, the controlled national economy, necessitated by war, worked out a drastic leveling down of our social structure. For the rationing of daily necessities as well as for the general regimentation of the people's lives, the neighborhood cooperative system, which had once flourished under the Tokugawa Shogunate regime, was revived, although in greatly modified form. The government ordered the people throughout the country to group themselves into units called "neighborhood societies," each unit to be formed by some dozen families grouped together solely on the basis of "residential adjacency."

This had remarkable effects on the people in big cities like Tokyo, where residential sections were not clearly marked and classified as in many towns of the Western countries, and where rich mansions had tenement houses and petty tradesmen's shops clustered around them in any old way. When the order was issued, there was no time to shuffle around and choose one's neighbors. Everyone was caught where he was.

The neighborhood society to which my family belonged consisted of eleven families headed by two peers. Then came a war millionaire, a government official, a beautiful widow, a steward and a chauffeur—both in service to a rich baron—a semi-government official, a gardener, a factory worker, and a school teacher—my husband. There were some minor changes in the membership during the course of the several years, but most of the families remained permanent until or very near the end of the war.

These member families took semi-yearly turns in officiating as society president and air-defense captain, and met usually at the president's house as often as was necessary. With the aggravation of the war situation, food and fuel questions became acute, and air-raid drills and defense installations more and more urgent. The member families had to work in compact cooperation. Moreover, the increasing difficulty in traffic and communication made it impossible for any family to depend, in an emergency, on the cooperation of its scattered relatives. A next-door neighbor became much more reliable than a brother only a mile away. And thus the traditional Japanese family sentiment for turning to relatives in case of need was superseded by a democratic way of not feeling ashamed to disclose one's plight to non-relatives, and to ask for their help.

So the people, particularly the housewives in my neighborhood society, became very intimate with each other, and many times a day they stepped through their broken garden fences and called at each other's unrepaired kitchen doors to pass on the ward-office's circulars, or to borrow a spoonful of sugar, a pint of soy-bean sauce or an ounce of dried bonito chips.

As a whole, we got along very congenially because we had so much in common to complain about, all practically being servantless and occupied equally with patching clothes, cooking meals and chopping firewood. It just happened that most of the wives of my neighborhood society were women in their ripe forties—efficient, experienced, sociable and tactful. So despite the wide range of difference in the occupation and social standing of their husbands, these women made themselves perfectly agreeable neighbors to each other. There were two young wives in their early twenties, who more or less grouped themselves with the unmarried girls of the neighborhood. The elderly group were very thoughtful and helpful to these girls, but somehow they were overcritical, or so it appeared at least to me, about the lighting conditions of the houses of the young people, for they often talked among themselves about the "indecently bright use"—from the standpoint of the anti-airraid precautions—or "improperly early extinction" of the electric lights by these recently married couples. We had become quite sensitive by that time to the slightest luminosity of night lights.

As a matter of technical necessity, everyone in our neighborhood society knew everyone else's family conditions—ages, dispositions, occupations, amounts of war-bonds bought, income taxes and other taxes, if any, health conditions, temporary absences, school and labor service conditions of every member from the family head to the last baby, or the baby due to arrive in so many months. And most important of all, everyone had to know the plan and interior of everyone else's house, so that should any house be bombed, all the neighborhood could instantly run to the spot—water pail, broom and shovel in hand. In a word, a heterogeneous section of Japanese society, represented in my neighborhood society, was being compounded and compacted into a tightly knit unit of the new social order that was rising.

The most interesting thing about this new social order was the way that little children caught on to the idea. They took it for granted that things were to be distributed equally among all members. They often gathered stones and flowers in our gardens and distributed them to all the houses. One day two little boys stood at my door with a basketful of dragon-flies and proudly said, "Today you shall have rationing of these animals, one for each house!"

"Why, you have two umbrellas," said a little girl, peeping into the veranda of my nextdoor neighbor. "Give me one because I haven't got any."

Our most distinguished neighbor was Baron K, who was the eighteenth son, so I was told, of one of the most central figures of the Meiji Restoration. He was related to a great many powerful peers and to the Imperial Family, too. His old, many-gabled, many-corridored mansion was so spacious that even its entrance hall alone would have contained my tiny three-room house with ample space to spare. His drawing-room, which seemed to me a mile off from the entrance hall, and where we often met and talked about potato rations and how to cut down the consumption of charcoal through the winter, was surrounded with huge sliding doors, painted with gold dust. The Baron was well over fifty, but life had not hardened him a bit. He was good to everyone and had almost childlike shyness, joviality and sociableness. He seemed to occupy a great deal of his time with gardening, fishing and good wines, but showed great willingness to work with the rest of the people and was always the first to volunteer for hard work.

· 13 ·

"Think of the time not long ago when we commoners salaamed flat by the roadside when the Baron's father rode along in a grand cavalcade!" the historical-minded of us said to each other, and felt a sort of gratification at the great change.

The Baroness, a fair, plump, charming lady, was remarkably efficient and practical, and capably made up for the impracticality of her husband. She talked to the women of the community in a very democratic way, while some of the commoners' wives began to use some words from the vocabulary of the elite speech which is clearly marked in the Japanese language. The wife of the older son, an oval-faced, placid-featured girl, was a typical beauty of the Japanese nobility. She always served tea at our community meetings. Both these ladies came from famous historical families. The two boys of the family, a naval lieutenant and a university student, were away most of the time.

Another titled member of our community was Viscount M, head of an old *daimyo* family, who lived with his bank clerk son, his daughter-in-law and two grandchildren in his modestly aristocratic mansion. He was a charming, scholarly gentleman with plenty of old books in his library. He wore Western clothes all the time, but evidently could not afford to wear leather shoes every day, so he walked around in wooden clogs over his Japanese-socked feet. He told me that he had been a "fellow scholar" to the Crown Prince, later Emperor Taisho, and had studied Chinese classics with him under my husband's grandfather.

The cotton merchant was undoubtedly the richest member,

considering his stocks of cotton textiles now commanding fabulous prices. He had his office downtown, and had built his present house since the outbreak of the China War. Everything was new and handsome in this beautiful home. He had six children, and his dimpled little wife managed the household without the help of a single maid. His youngest boy had a habit of picking bits of charcoal and wooden splinters off the street and taking them to his mamma for fuel.

The cotton merchant had three nice-looking tenant houses in a corner of his grounds. The beautiful widow, the young government official—who was the beloved son-in-law of one of the biggest generals of the Japanese Army, and the official of the National Textiles Distributing Organ were their respective tenants.

Baron O's steward and chauffeur lived next door to our house, and daily commuted to their master's mansion on the other edge of the city. Their master was one of the biggest *zaibatsu* of Japan and lived as grandly as any millionaire in the world, but the steward, who had charge of the key of the master's household vault, and the chauffeur, to whom the lordly Baron daily entrusted his life, both lived in shabby little houses with apparent contentment, like humble, faithful Japanese servants. The chauffeur had two boys, the older of whom was in China.

At the community council meetings, the chauffeur always sat lumpishly in the corner, and hardly spoke. Whenever he had to say something he stammered so badly that no one understood him very well. He appeared completely wooden. But once in charge of his master's car, he was as bright and self-confident as the grand machine itself, and as precise, too. I remembered having seen in America some chauffeurs employed by rich households who acted stodgily and even gruffly toward their employers, and now had my observation double-checked that employers the world over preferred the safety of their lives to pleasant mannered servants.

The chauffeur's wife was a vivacious, energetic, hard-working woman. She had turned the tiny, stony space at the back of her kitchen into a thriving patch of potatoes, turnips and broom grass. When her broom grass turned red and hardened in autumn, she dried it and made several brooms out of the crop. When she presented me with one of them, I felt the world suddenly brighten up. I had been without a broom for some time, for none were on sale any more and there had been no way, except by raking with my own fingers, to remove the dust and dirt that had accumulated in my house. Until then I had not realized what comfort a single little broom afforded a human soul.

The factory worker lived next to the chauffeur. He was a skilled mechanic and worked in a big munitions factory. He had recently married and lived in what seemed to me an enviably comfortable way.

The gardener, the last member of our neighborhood society, lived in what used to be the porter's lodge standing at the end of Baron K's azalea-lined driveway. He was formerly Baron K's family gardener but did not work for him now. Moreover, he had had to give up his profession altogether—since no one cared any more for potted trees and ornamental stones—

and was now working as a clerk in a food-distributing office. His dilapidated house was filled with his five children and lines of diapers.

It was the extreme uncertainty of the war situation that made these most heterogeneous elements of our community cooperate very willingly with each other on an absolutely equal footing. Food and other necessities, rationed by the government and received through the medium of the neighborhood society, were rated strictly on a per capita or family basis. Anything procured by black market or bribery was carefully hidden away. "We are all equals," was the idea publicly respected and in force at this time.

In dingy trousers and tight-sleeved coats, all the men and women of our community, including titled lords and ladies, practiced relaying water pails and carrying stretchers, and shouldered loads of lumber and earth in community labor service. The jovial Baron K, who evidently used to hand out great sums of money to *geisha* girls, seemed really to enjoy the "free" company of the young girls of the neighborhood and of Mrs. Y, the charming widow. Evidently young women in trousers had a strange attractiveness, which had passed unnoticed in the decorative geisha costumes.

Although Mrs. Y was not popular among the housewives of the community, I loved to look at this tall, slim, lovely figured woman in her early forties, always perfectly dressed and groomed. Apparently she had plentiful supplies of food. She kept an extremely efficient housemaid, and even two white Pekingese dogs, although she had three good-looking children of her own who should have kept her busy and happy enough. She was gossiped about as being on intimate terms with more than one important naval officer, and when she moved away to a seaside town a few months before the destruction came to our neighborhood, everyone wondered about the handsome motor-truck that made many trips for her abundant evacuation baggage, including her whining, yelping pets. Private use of motor-trucks by that time was limited only to a privileged few. At any rate, the fair, breezy lady supplied the neighborhood with lively conversation, and quite unintentionally diverted the people out of their strenuous daily routine. In fact she was the only elite of our community.

Our neighborhood society was but one example of the general levelling down then in process throughout the social structure of Japan. All of us now stood on equal terms as faithful soldiers of the Divine Emperor. The military hierarchy with its "elite" existed tactically but never socially, so the argument went.

Food shortages became keenly felt by our family from the second year of the Pacific War. A family like ours, whose economic foundation consisted solely of the meager teaching salaries of my husband, and the small fees for my sporadic writing and translation work, and which stood completely outside the "wartime military-industrial-agricultural setup" or the country, suffered severely from the food and clothing shortages. As for clothes, we could go about in multi-patched, nondescript garments, although it was never a pleasant sensation to wonder whether your clothes would properly stay on your back. But food was imperative. Practically all my time now was spent in running from one food rationing office to another, going out into the country for fresh vegetables, and then cooking these costly foodstuffs with meagerly rationed fuel.

Presently all the children, except Kazuko, were recruited to labor service—the boys in munition factories, and airfield construction, and the girl of thirteen to a job peeling mica and polishing lenses. They worked under the same conditions as regular workers, and the boys learned to smoke, and picked up other habits of grown-up factory men.

"Smoking makes you forget hunger," the boys told me.

Their wages, which were figured at the students' labor service rate and not according to the regular workers' pay, went to their schools which, after deducting their tuition and incidental expenses—although there was hardly any more school work going on—handed over the remainder to the parents.

Strangely enough, the last year and a half or so of the hectic war period was the only time in my married life when I did not have to worry about money. The children earned wages. My husband also got rations of food and cigarettes when these were distributed to his students. Our joint incomes were just enough to pay for our rationed food, government-controlled house rent, and absolutely necessary incidentals. There was nothing else openly obtainable, all shops in the country having been publicly closed. So if we did not get involved in the black market, money weighed very lightly in our daily life.

Black market transactions required cash in hand, or stores of goods—neither of which my family possessed. So we stoically put aside our desires for tasty foods. For clothing material, for which the government distributed coupons on a per capita basis, we could not afford to spend a cent. Moreover, with these coupons we could only obtain silks, or fabrics of the newly introduced synthetic material called "the staple fibre." Cotton and woolen were now forbidden articles. This "staple fibre," however, was hardly more durable than paper, and had a strange appeal to locusts, who nibbled at it. So I clothed my children with the shirts and pants discarded by the families of some of my friends, and also with clothes made over of my cotton, woolen and pongee kimonos. I myself went around in *mompé* * overalls of whatever silk crepe or brocade I found lying idle in my chest of drawers.

The government-rationed food was not enough to keep one alive and going, and more and more, sweet and Irish potatoes, often mildewed, and flour—frequently of a strange taste— came to be substituted for our rice and barley. But no complaint whatsoever was taken up at the rationing offices. Soon it became absolutely necessary for me to obtain some unrationed food supplies directly from farmers.

I went on a buying-out trip nearly once a week. Each week I had to travel farther from the city, because the distance and the prices varied inversely for this rural traffic. Moreover, my visits to country farms had to be financed by gifts in kind— cotton goods and soap, in particular. Farmers, more than any

---

* *Mompé* is a costume consisting of a pair of loose trousers and a tight-sleeved coat, worn by women of northern Japan in winter. It was adopted during the war by women and old men of the entire country.

one else, scorned money. But I had none of these attractive gifts to court farmers' favors with, so I usually cooperated with a neighboring housewife, who had stores of cotton pieces and sewing thread. Her husband, once the manager of a sewing factory, was now an official of the National Textiles Distributing Organ. Out of the material offered by her I made shirts and trousers on my sewing machine—necessity had taught me to sew these things in my own style, and Japanese farmers were never too particular about cut and style—and she and I usually went to the country together. Sometimes I took sewing orders directly from farmers, to whom I was known as "the tailor-woman."

But if I was so fortunate as to have enough food in the house to feed the family at least for tomorrow, I would put aside all earthly cares and household labor and, book in hand, crawl into my bed, which I often left spread on the floor instead of putting it away in the closet every morning. There was no use to clean a house that might be bombed at any time. It was, moreover, downright foolish to do unnecessary work and get myself hungry when food was so hard to get. A good housewife should be as lazy as possible and eat as little as possible. So at any time of the day I lay in bed, with perfectly good excuses, and read stories. In this way I picked up a few hours of complete leisure now and then in the midst of surging and towering war-worries, and buried myself in the world of fiction—of good, solid stories, which never before in my previous married life of hard domestic struggles had I had time or inclination to start reading. But all these years books had been, and were still, lying, standing and leaning everywhere in our house and I could now pick out of them a dozen fascinating novels at once. I read Japanese translations of *Vanity Fair, Ivanhoe, The Forsyte Saga, Jean Christophe, Gone with the Wind, The Good Earth* and many others of Pearl Buck's stories, and many contemporary Chinese writers, as well as Japanese authors, both classical and contemporary.

I felt as if I was being lulled in a luxurious dream-boat in the midst of a sea of troubles, and told myself that when there were too many things to worry about and too much hard work to do, the best thing was to stop worrying and working altogether. Suddenly, in the midst of these moments of sweet peace and oblivion, an air-raid alarm would shriek, and back I would come to the world of hopeless reality.

4. The Bombing of Tokyo

Our government encouraged the inhabitants of big cities to move into the country, first because there was more food there and second, because of the imminent bombing by American planes. But only a small percentage of our city population actually moved away. In our overcrowded islands, even rural districts had no surplus land or much surplus food for such evacuées to pick up. Rich people with country homes, or money enough to pay an exorbitant rent for a room in a flee-infested farmhouse on a remote mountainside, and heaps of silk kimonos with which to please country women and coax from them rice and sweet potatoes, were the first to evacuate, carrying truck-loads of baggage with them. But the best most people could do was to send away their old and their young into the care of their country relatives—if they had any. Some school children were taken *en masse* by their teachers to country temples.

For the masses of people who could not evacuate the cities expected to be bombed soon, the government offered to trans-port at special rates a certain number of packages per household and deliver them to whatever safe custodians were designated.

My family had very little to do with evacuation problems. Neither my husband nor I had country relatives except some distant cousins in western Japan, far from Tokyo. We could send away some of our possessions, but our possessions consisted chiefly of books—tons of dictionaries and encyclopedias, clas-sics of various countries, Japanese and Chinese in particular, modern Japanese literature and children's books. The modern style books were too heavy to handle, and the frail Chinese and Japanese volumes would not stand the rough evacuation process. So we decided to send away nothing and to stay on where we were, ready to face whatever lot might befall us. We could not imagine that our neighborhood, quite withdrawn from the pop-ulous heart of the city, would ever be bombed.

We did not know yet what "being bombed" was really like. The attacks of the Doolittle fliers had not had much effect on the people. We followed the orders of the air-defense guidance officers gruntedly and apathetically.

I remember it was early in November 1944, that the first American reconnaissance plane—perhaps two planes—rode over the city of Tokyo. It was a clear late autumn day, and in the blue and gold sky the uncanny speck floated long and undisturbed, far above the range of our anti-aircraft guns, while Tokyo traffic and business stopped, and held its breath in ominous, dead silence.

A few weeks later bombing began. It began with a daytime invasion of a few dozen B-29's dropping bombs on one of the biggest aircraft factories in the Tokyo area. For the first time the inhabitants of Tokyo heard the peculiar booming of the four-motored giant bombers sailing over in successive formations, and the thuds and explosions of heavy bombs hurled from 10,000 meter heights. That evening we were told that many high-school girls working as student hands in that factory had perished among crowds of regular workers in flimsily built underground shelters.

Raid after raid followed. Fleets of mighty bombers visited the capital by day and by night. We soon discovered that night attacks were mostly directed at residential sections. We now slept with heavy clothes on and our feet covered with thick socks so that we could run out of the house at any time of the night. The day after the first night raid, I think it was, I met a friend on the street. "Do you know what I discovered this morning?" the wan-faced friend said. "I saw streaks of rainwater wetting the wall of my drawing-room. 'How strange!' I thought and looked up and what should I see there but a footlong incendiary bomb stuck right through the ceiling!" The air-defense officer of her district succeeded in dislodging the unexploded bomb safely, and saved her beautiful home. Both she and I shuddered at the narrow escape. But very soon we became toughened to it.

We were quite certain that on Christmas Eve we would not be bombed, and slept with just a little more sense of security than usual. In fact we had a brief Christmas truce with the "Bees," as the familiar B-29's had come to be called. We eagerly hoped that the U. S. airmen at Saipan would celebrate another holiday on New Year's Eve. But just about midnight, when whatever temple bells had been saved from being melted and turned into bullets and bombs were ringing out the old year, together with all the human sins of the past, came the alarm. "Of all things, to be burnt out naked into the New Year street!" we said to each other, trembling with fear and cold. The New Year was so dear, so sacred and inviolable to Japanese sentiment. A small number of planes strolled over the city and dropped a few bombs which, however, seemed to have peculiarly noisy sound effects. Our radio signal stations caught a "Happy New Year!" greeting from the triumphantly retreating Bees.

"Can we sleep tonight?" became the most serious daily question in Tokyo. One night when it began to snow heavily, we were delighted, because we thought the weather too wet for incendiary bombs. But the alerting sirens began to hoot in the middle of the night, and then came the alarm. We ran out into snow a foot deep, heard the muffled booms of the Bees, then the volleys of explosions in the distance. Presently the sky lighted up, and the snow around us turned a deep pink. The next morning we learned that large sections in the heart of the city had been incinerated, snow and all.

A few days later, a report came to me by quick relays through my family circle that a young cousin of ours had been burnt out on that snowy night and lost everything—her rich bridal trousseau, and her husband's handsome house filled with beautiful things inherited from his deceased parents, two childless uncles and titled grandmother—all vanished overnight! The young girl, with her husband—both in mud-covered air-defense outfits and each carrying nothing but an emergency bag on the back, which by the prescription of the air-defense guidance office, contained a few handfuls of rice, a pair of candles, a match box, a towel, bandage material and a few other things—appeared the next morning at her parents' door, looking like a pair of beggars. I knew exactly how Uncle Yasusaburo looked and felt at that moment. He had put so much money, labor and loving care into collecting exquisite kimonos and beautiful furniture for his daughter's wedding two and a half years before.

"Of all people, she would be the first victim, the richest kimono-owner of us all!" we said to each other, and cried and laughed in hysterical fits. But we did not have time to condole long on her loss.

The raids steadily increased in frequency and in extent, coming to a climax on March 10, 1945. It was a pitch-dark night, with a strong west wind howling. The invading force was of unprecedented size, and the bombing proportionally greater. The red glow that spread over the southeastern horizon quickly bulged up and filled the entire sky, so that even where we were, on the opposite edge of the city, an eerie pink light settled on the earth and clearly lit up the deep-lined faces of the awe-struck people. The burning seemed to go on all the night.

When dawn came, practically the entire downtown areas of Tokyo were full of embers containing numberless charred bodies. In the low sections of the city, comparatively recently reclaimed from the sea, where water oozed out only a foot below the surface of the ground, the inhabitants were unable to build underground shelters. They were helplessly hunted out by the raging flames and perished in tens of thousands.

Some households in my neighborhood society became suddenly crowded, because burnt-out relatives had been taken in. The cotton merchant, whose downtown office had been swept away, now had his brother's family living with him. With a shudder his wife told me that these relatives, when the bombing came, took refuge in the basement of a nearby concrete theatre, but somehow not feeling safe there, they went out again, and ducking many flames and throwing off whatever clothes had caught fire, they ran and ran until dawn came and the fires subsided. Later they found that the big theatre had been burnt, or rather baked to ashes with hundreds of refugees caught in the basement. It seems that the basements of modern buildings tempted and betrayed many other bomb-and-flame-hunted people on that night.

The big worker-type man, who had come to live with the gardener, told me how he had survived. In the confusion he got separated from his family and while running wildly in search of them, he was trapped by the flames. He ran into a school playground where many people had taken refuge. Presently the air got very hot and the asphalt pavement of the playground began to stick and smoke. Fire was on all sides and the people began to stamp and then jump up and down because they could not stand still on the hot, melting asphalt. One by one, however, they stopped jumping and dropped to the ground never to rise again, "Human beings die so easily and so quietly," he observed to me. He and just a few other strongly-built men continued jumping and wriggling all the night.

He still limped badly and had both his hands heavily bandaged. A young girl took care of him. "Did you find your family?" I asked him. "Only one daughter," he said.

At that time my husband was in a hospital, where he heard the report of the destruction in the same air-raid of the school founded by his grandfather 75 years before. He had developed a rather serious case of tympanitis, after serving as our community air-defense captain and having to get up almost every night and go round cracking thick ice in our community water-tanks. It was an exceptionally cold winter with plenty of ice and snow. I had to go to the hospital at least every other day, to bring food and heating material to my husband, because the hospital gave the patients whatever medical care it could, but was unable to attend to anything else. I took whatever traffic lines were running but often had to walk all the three-mile distance, shouldering my loads of charcoal and steaming pot and jostling through crowds of refugees. The hospital was filled with burnt people.

At the hospital, in the street, and in my neighborhood, people in dirty clothes now talked and talked, never caring whom they were talking to. They had got over the customary Japanese reserve and spoke to anyone around as though afraid that if they stopped they would lose contact with their fellow humans. And everyone had endless stories to tell about the last big night-raid.

The March 10th event was probably the greatest horror the people of Tokyo underwent during the war. It was too terrible to excite any personal hatred in the hunted people against the bombing enemy. We were profoundly impressed and mentally numbed, utterly passive. The citizens of recovered Tokyo today still talk about it with awe, but if any hatred—which is an active personal feeling—mingles with their terrible memories, it is only a hatred of modern warfare and not of the American people.

After that horrible night-raid, the residents of Tokyo began to think of evacuation in good earnest. A single motor-truck trip now cost 10,000 yen and upward, besides involving huge presents of clothes and food to the driver, and the purchase of precious gasoline through the black market. Those who could afford the cost hurried away with their truck-loads of possessions, but the poor masses simply carried off whatever of their scanty property they could manage to shoulder. Any principal railway station around the capital swarmed with these carriers of "evacuation goods." A thick line of man-or-woman-drawn carts and hand-pushed trundles, loaded beyond capacity, stretched a good mile from the checking office, each sender

awaiting his turn for hours and even days, all the while guarding his baggage with the closest possible vigilance. Inside and
outside the station building, gathered crowds of dirty people,
most of whom carried huge loads on their back—big bundles
of bedding quilts, chests of drawers, piles of wallets, household
utensils from a wash-tub to a bamboo dipper. These bundles
looked as if they were walking by themselves, for so huge were
they in proportion to the size of the carriers to whose backs
they were bound tightly with thick strings, very often made of
silk *obi,* that the carriers could hardly breathe, to say nothing
of bending their bodies even slightly. Nearly half of the crowds
were women—brown, wrinkled women, and chubby-cheeked
little girls all hauling loads bigger than themselves. And indeed, anyone, having anything to carry on his back, felt sincerely happy, for countless burnt-out refugees, stripped of all
earthly possessions, lay like discarded rags in the corners of the
station hall.

Night-raids, which generally aimed at burning residential
houses and in which we could not well observe the behavior of
the attacking planes, filled us with much more fear and sense
of uncertainty. Daytime raids were somewhat different.

The most magnificent spectacle I ever beheld was the host
of day invaders I met on one of my country buying trips. It
was a bright, clear day and from the morning I was filled with
misgiving, for usually the Bees came on such a day. But rain,
fire, bombs or whatever else might be falling, I had to travel
into the country to get food supplies. I went out with my usual
companion, Mrs. T.

When the train pulled into the station on the other side of the river that marked the northwestern border of the city, we heard a long-drawn out whooping of sirens. "It's only the preliminary alerting," we said self-comforting. "We can't tell yet which of the hundred cities of Japan is going to be hit." The train stood still and presently sharp peals sounded. All the passengers got off and ran to the shelters in the station compound, taking with them only those of their possessions that they could carry in their hands and still run. But these public shelters were too few. Many ran out of the station into the town street. The sirens had finished their ten weird diminuendos, and in the dead silence that now reigned over heaven and earth came a distant boom.

"Run quick into our shelter!" a man's voice shouted. Mrs. T. and I gratefully accepted the invitation.

In the eastern sky loomed a flight, another flight and yet another of B-29's. Keeping a 10,000 meter height and trailing white streamers of exhaust gas, they sailed in perfect formation through the blue-gold sky. To a purely aesthetic eye they looked like shawls of pearly fish riding through the seas of the universe. But to the humans, exposed to their potent wrath, they were the Almighty in every respect. A pious American Japanese lady had once remarked that they looked exactly like angels, more like angels than any of the painted angels of the great masters. But to the Buddhist-Japanese, "angels" meant soft, soothing and often voluptuous creatures. So, completely apart from traditional religious associations, the ethereal beauty of the mighty bombers was Destiny itself to the people trembling below them.

Suddenly came z-z-z-z-z-z, a sound like that of ocean billows breaking on a sandy beach. The people, who had been enticed to the mouths of their dugouts by the sheer beauty of the high-flying planes, simultaneously pulled in their heads. Then came heavy rolling sounds like thunderclaps, mingled with ponderous thuds vibrating into the earth. Now sharp volleys of anti-aircraft guns joined in from the ground.

The radio in the neighboring houses, in a firm, composed masculine voice, was reporting on the movement of the raiding enemy. The downtown business centre of Tokyo was the main target.

The process of splashing the earth with showers of incendiary bullets in rhythmic rumbles of ocean breakers, and hurling heavy bombs, each pounding with a fatal thud into the depth of the globe, was repeated by each flight of planes. On almost every raid it seemed to us, the American planes brought over new kinds of bombs and shells, which behaved differently in sound effects from those used the last time. The unaccustomed noises intensified the terrors and thrills of each new invasion.

Most Tokyo people had learned by this time that when the Bees were flying at 10,000 meters, the moment any one of them was exactly overhead was the danger-time according to the law of projectiles; otherwise none of the lordly bombers could hurt you. And once out of danger, one could not help but feel the thrill of the mighty fight.

"Look, the Japanese planes are chasing them!" some voices shouted. We popped our heads out of the dugout again just in time to see one of the Japanese fighters, a black midget against a glistening flock of sailing swans, make a big circle and a swift dash against one of them. The next moment it spitted black smoke and came down fast, its wings broken like a mutilated grasshopper. "Oh, oh, oh!" the spectators groaned.

"Look at that Bee!" came a shout again. One of the big American planes was making a fast descent, wrapped up in a gigantic column of smoke and emitting a thundrous hissing noise. "Hurrah!" the people shouted, amidst the booming of exploding bombs and volleying anti-aircraft guns.

Huge masses of smoke began to bulge in the distance, while each of the flying echelons, after discharging bombs at the planned points, made a sweeping eastward turn, and still in perfect order, some eighty in all of the majestic planes sailed away over the Pacific Ocean, the sun shining golden on their triumphant wings.

Just one of them, however, began to lag behind and come down lower and lower. It remained a dark speck even after all its companions had merged into the void.

All of a sudden I realized that there were some people—the idea of enemy or friends did not occur to me—riding in that lagging and falling plane. "What would be the sensation of the people on that plane?" the spectators observed, generally in a sympathetic tone.

It was hard to interpret modern scientific warfare of this kind in terms of personal human feelings. Once out of the danger zone, even women and children could watch an air fight overhead with the thrill of cheering at some magnificent sport. No human suffering was visible at the moment. It was the action of mere machines—the fighting and destruction of insentient, glorious winged creatures of man's making—whose cruel effects on humanity were of later consequence and inconceivable subtlety.

Moreover, to the Japanese people, who had no effective machines with which to combat the hosts of powerful American planes, the bombing was exactly like their old game of thunderbolt, only played in dead earnest. After the descent of each thunderbolt, the survivors heaved a sigh of the sincerest gratitude, an instinctive, selfish gratitude for the momentary favor of Blind Chance. It afforded an infinite sensation of thrill and exultation because you played the game while standing tiptoe on a tight-drawn death line.

Long peals of sirens came at last, signalling the lifting of the warning and bringing back the sweetness of life to the survivors of a death sentence. For the first time, like the rest of the people, I became conscious of our earthly surroundings. I noticed that there were some dozen refugees filling the small air-raid shelter, at the entrance of which I had been squatting with Mrs. T.

"Lucky we still have heads on our shoulders," said the people as they came out one by one. Then a little girl of ten or so emerged carrying a baby on her back and followed by a tiny boy, each peacefully nibbling on a steamed sweet potato. Evidently the bombing did not make much impression on the children as they had been quietly munching goodies at the bottom of the dugout all the time. The boy only said, blinking his eyes, that it was so good to see the blue sky and the bright sunshine again. They all trotted off after their young mother, who carried a handsome cupboard tied on her back.

"We have wasted four hours here, thanks to the wicked Bees," grumbled Mrs. T and I, thinking of the tedious trip still ahead and fearing that we could not possibly get home before dark.

"You are buying-outers, aren't you?" A farmer suddenly spoke to us and offered to sell us some flour and vegetables, if we walked with him to his farm. We were astonished because we had never been very hospitably received by a farmer in any of our previous food-traffic adventures. But it was just the moment where everybody was most benignly disposed toward his fellow humans in the sheer joy of being alive. We were only too happy to walk with the farmer two and a half miles along a dusty country road, for in any buying-out expedition, walking that distance was a matter of course, since farmers near a railway station were completely "city-spoiled."

The kind host, after treating two tired and hungry women with a cup of tea and a plateful of steamed toro roots, took out two big basketfuls of good Irish and sweet potatoes, measured some rice and flour into the small bags each of us had brought against any such luck, and gave us some burdock roots and onions in addition. His charge was surprisingly low even taking into consideration the cotton shirt we had presented to him.

With a hearty smile we each shouldered a load of 50 pounds, grasped an additional big bundle, and triumphantly began to walk back. Shortly, however, we began to feel as if we were a team of oxen stretching their necks in the sole desire of reaching home at the earliest possible time and being relieved of the burdens cutting into their backs. Despite our great maternal love, and joy of accomplishment for it, we had to acknowledge the beastly status of such labor, and in mute patience we plodded along.

The train was crowded as usual and there was no way of getting on it through any of the overflowing decks with such heavy loads on our backs. Following my companion's and many other people's examples, I pushed in my big bundles through one of the train windows and jumped on the window myself, feeling most grateful for my tight *mompé* trousers. During my desperate struggle to climb in, I felt a strong hand supporting and pushing up my feet, but when after getting into the train I turned back to say thank you for the kind help, the train had already started and no man was seen standing on the platform.

It was not the first time I had received a helping hand from an unknown man. Under the stress of war, some Japanese men had cast away their peculiar show of indifference toward women and had become quite chivalrous.

5. The Last Days

The visits of the B-29's became less frequent in Tokyo, while other cities were bombed one after another. But whenever they did come to the capital, their number and destructive power was increasingly potent. The coastal bombardments of U. S. ships and the rumors of the landing plans of U. S. forces on the

Japanese homeland now sent the people of Tokyo, as well as of many other coastal cities, flying into remote mountain districts, abandoning most of their possessions, and squeezing themselves into whatever emergency hospitality they could procure for love or money from the hardy hillmen. I saw many evacuées shouldering their things in bags made of women's silk brocade obi, for good canvas rucksacks had become the dearest and rarest articles in the country.

Everywhere in the doomed city were discarded houses and furniture. My children, who had always longed to have a piano in the house, could now own any number of them just for the picking, for all our evacuating friends said to us, "Take anything you like out of our house." Only we, like the rest of the people, had no means of transportation except our own hands and shoulders. No one would even take a piano left by the roadside, unless he was in dire need of fuel. And indeed, handsome desks and cabinets and beautiful chests of drawers were put on sale for ten yen apiece, for firewood. The moment the war ceased, however, their prices literally increased a thousand times. The sense of private property had been almost completely removed from everyone's mind.

"Pick anything off anyone's house before it is bombed and burnt," was the guiding idea of the time. The usual greeting when you met a friend on the street was simply, "Not burnt out yet?" Nothing else seemed to matter. Our family, who had had to put aside all thought of evacuation, simply hoped that peace would be concluded before complete destruction came to the country.

In our neighborhood community, the two titled families were the first to evacuate. Then Mrs. Y in her grand style, and the gardener with five children in his bullock cart, moved away, while the cotton millionaire sent away his wife and younger children. There were some more minor cases of moving out, but the vacancies were quickly filled up by burnt-out people so that our community population rather increased than decreased. "They won't bomb this secluded suburban locality," we said to ourselves comfortingly.

There were one or two rather extensive night-raids and several daytime attacks on Tokyo during the interval between March 10th and the end of May when the big finishing-up raids came. On the nights of May 23rd and 25th, sheets of flames covered the still inhabited parts of Tokyo. By the morning of May 26th, 1945, the city, once a vast metropolis of some eight million inhabitants, had been practically wiped out.

By that time we had been fighting fire for sixty-five hours on the run. Our anti-aircraft guns had long ceased to operate. The great bombers now came down as low as they pleased, deafening our ears with their thundering boom and showing their huge contours against the glow of burning houses. The incendiary bombs dropped by some planes of the last formation in the invading host of May 25th, descended in rattling and hissing bunches on the edge of our neighborhood.

Our water faucets did not work any more. There were a number of wells around, but of what use was hand-pumped well-water against torrents of flaming oil? Our community people, who had buried the most indispensable of their possessions underground, now wetted their clothes against the flying sparks and stood idly watching the flames spread. The wind was blowing in every direction and we simply prayed that it would not blow the flames over our house. The north was comparatively dark, so we thought we could escape in that direction without being trapped by fire. Our new neighbors, who had been burnt out already once or twice, were so frightened and harassed that, hugging their scanty possessions and each family gathering closely together, they fled without waiting for the fire-captain's instructions. Some hardy fighters made many trips, carrying chests of drawers and huge bundles of bed-quilts on their backs, which they deposited in the corner of Baron K's spacious garden. My husband and I simply watched the scene.

Our little girl, carrying some of her clothes and school textbooks on her back, had already fled with our nextdoor neighbors. Since my husband was the air-defense sub-captain of our community, he and I went round to see the houses under our charge. Suddenly a huge column of flame sprung up on the edge of Baron K's big mansion and a whirlwind of sparks struck our faces. "Let's fly!" the fire captain cried. We all ran after him.

Even then I still hoped that our house might be saved by a sudden turn in the direction of the wind. We walked probably half a mile and finding a dark, cool place by the roadside, sat down. My husband and I sat there for an hour or so, completely mute, except that we said to each other that our little girl would be safe in the hands of our nextdoor neighbors, and that the grandmother and two older children—the older boy was then away from home on labor service—must have taken refuge safely somewhere with their neighbors.

Gradually the bright glow in the direction of our place began to pale. My husband and I noticed that all our companions had gone. We got up and walked back as fast as our heavy outfit and tired feet could carry us. When we turned the last corner, there we saw our house outlined in red-glowing embers, still keeping its original shape. "Burnt out after all!" I said to myself. Since I now saw it, I had to admit that my house had gone. The next moment the house collapsed to the ground. My husband, in a choked voice, said, "My books!"

Then I found that all our neighbors were absent-mindedly gazing on the embers of their houses. Our little girl came back with her companions. My husband found his mother and two older children, whose house, a quarter of a mile distant from ours, had been also burnt down. "Since we are all safe, what does the loss of things matter?" we said to each other.

Daylight gradually came with drizzling rain and disclosed the denuded neighborhood. The soot-covered, rain-soaked people looked as miserable as gutter rats. We could hardly recognize each other's worn faces. When, however, we began to talk and hear each other's familiar voices, a sense of continuity returned to our bewildered minds. We realized that we, who yesterday had comfortable houses to live in, were the same people who today were sitting amidst ashes and facing tomorrow.

We decided for the time being to take shelter against the rain in one of the houses left standing in the neighborhood like scattered islets in the seas of war-debris. There were a number of evacuated houses still standing not far from our place, one of which was offered for the use of my family. When the family got indoors and felt somewhat comforted, the grandmother began to weep. The three children followed suit, the two younger ones crying aloud. I felt bitter pain in my heart, for remorse gnawed within me at not having saved more of our possessions, at having been too wishfully optimistic and failing to deposit more things in our underground shelter when there was still time. I could not weep.

When not even a piece of paper, or a pair of chopsticks was obtainable on the market, the loss of even a single teapot was heart-breaking. The loss of all one's possessions meant a downright fall to animal life. In our dugout we had saved some bedding, quilts, clothing, food and books. These we carried on our backs in many trips to our new empty house. For a while there was plenty of firewood, for we could go back to our burnt house and pick up any number of charred beams and pillars. Chopping these big logs into pieces with a worn-out axe borrowed from a neighbor of our new abode, we burnt them in a tiny portable mud oven, distributed by the ward office, and cooked the rationed soy beans for three meals a day. Everyone, especially the women, got smudged with soot, but for many days we didn't take the trouble to acquire a looking-glass and see how we looked.

Our burnt house, though one of the smallest in the neighborhood, was the slowest to crumble into ashes, because it was filled up with books. For a week the books smoked in the daytime and glowed red at night. When they were completely incinerated, we found on the site layers upon layers of ashes of different colors. The Chinese books of the Sung and the Ming dynasty, with their softly-creamed paper and beautiful wood-printed scripts, had turned into glistening snow-white powder of the finest quality imaginable. The 17th century volumes of Japanese *noh* drama and more recent Japanese and Chinese books had become slightly yellowish-white. The modern books produced coarse ashes in various shades of dingy gray.

I filled a broken jar reclaimed from the debris with white ashes from the medieval books of Oriental poetry and took it to our new home. All our family found the ashes the cleanest possible tooth-powder. I put some of them in water and used the lye for washing.

We dug out of the rubble of our house whatever could be used in any way, for since nothing was obtainable now unless given for love, the ashes of one's own house were the only material resources left to a burnt-out house owner. Under the hot June sun we made many daily trips to the old site to dig. In fact, I went alone most of the time, because my husband and children still went to factories weekdays and Sundays. So while my mother-in-law stayed home, I worked among the debris. After removing the heaps of burnt and broken mud tiles which made up the thick uppermost layer, I poked into the finer inside ashes with a piece of broken and twisted gas pipe picked up on the spot.

First of all I looked for the heavy steel-coated trunk in which I had kept my husband's and my own best clothes. But I could not find a single trace of it. I had long been in the habit of keeping most of my kimonos in pawnbrokers' custody, and when in anticipation of the bombing of the city, the pawnbrokers of Tokyo closed their shops, I had sold my gold watch and a few other left-over pieces of jewelry and redeemed my pledges, some of them having been out of my chest of drawers for ten years. They were few in number, being the last pieces I had treasured through these years of financial struggles. I had designed the patterns and coloring of some of them myself. When finally reclaimed, I had given them a few loving strokes and put them in my trunk, foolishly hoping that its steel-coating would protect the contents from fire. But how completely it had disappeared, just a single piece of its brass fitting remaining in the ashes as a material reminder of the vanished treasures.

Remembering then my last knicknacks of jewelry, I looked for my mirror-stand, which I recognized by a handful of fine charcoal produced from the hard mulberry wood. But I found none of the ornamental pieces I had kept in its drawers, except the little silver cross—now turned dark purple—which I had bought at Ste. Genevieve's in Paris. By the silver cross lay an ugly, distorted lump of yellowish gray substance, which I could not identify until my nextdoor neighbor picked up a similar object and wonderingly showed it to me. "The mirror!" we said all at once, and looked at each other's soot-besmeared faces. It was my big, oval-shaped, steel-blue mirror, the only luxury I had possessed in the way of furniture.

My cupboard was a mess of broken china. The collection of the finest jewel-like porcelain my sister left with me before going into the country had been totally pulverized, while the pottery of cruder manufacture had stood the fire and shock miraculously well. From a foot-deep pile of ashes I reclaimed a tea-ceremony bowl of black glaze, a blue-glazed chopstick-stand, now turned a lovely reddish-purple, an old Chinese fig-urine, and an earthen bell, all intact in shape and more beautiful than ever in color. These pottery pieces and a few cast-iron pots were the only things that came out whole and usable. The silver things were covered with ugly stains and were badly torn, cop-per and aluminum pots were flattened and softened like dough, and glassware had completely vanished.

Digging went on everywhere throughout the ruined areas. People in rags haunting the ashes of their old homes presented a pitiful, weird scene indeed. Some of our old neighbors found evacuated houses to move into like my family, or were given shelter by friends, but many preferred living in the debris, be-cause they had built solid underground shelters and saved a good deal of their possessions in them. They had no means of carrying these things to places of safety, so they lived on the spot and kept guard over them. By and by they built huts with burnt iron sheets, rusted bicycles, ripped telephone wire and whatever else they could collect on the spot. Thus over the wilderness of rubble there arose a colony of huts on the sites where our houses had once stood with wooded gardens around them.

The wastelands of war debris extended over the ruins of Tokyo, and everywhere hut-dwellers formed colonies and dug and poked into the ashes, which were practically the only re-sources of life for them. In many spots, particularly in the downtown districts, refugees wandered distractedly over the wilderness and pried into the rubble for the bones of their loved ones.

My family were lucky indeed to have found a house to live in. In the new house we found a good amount of furniture left by the former occupants, and with the bedding, clothes and kitchen utensils we had saved or reclaimed from the ashes, we were able to live at a bare subsistence rate at least during the summer. What we missed most seriously in these circumstances was a radio receiver, for sirens still hooted for daily air-raid alarms, but since we didn't know the movement of the raiding planes, we imagined the worst possibilities and became extremely nervous. Tokyo was not bombed after May 25th, but many neighboring towns were destroyed in close succession, and we were in constant fear of the familiar B-29's visiting our ruins and wiping the last trace of life out of them.

The day Yokohama was bombed has remained clearly in my memory. It was a cloudy day in early June. I was walking through the war debris to the East Asia Office in the hope of seeing a friend of mine there and asking him if there was by any chance a plane flying to Hongkong or even to Shanghai in the near future. I was doing this errand on behalf of a Chinese friend of mine.

Shortly after the bombing of Tokyo began, I saw one day at the post-office in my neighborhood a beautiful young girl desperately struggling with her scanty Japanese vocabulary. Taking her for a *nisei*, I spoke to her in English. Her sad, tight face suddenly brightened up and she poured forth her troubles in torrents of beautiful, British-accented English.

She was married to a nisei Japanese-Canadian, who was working as an interpreter to the Japanese Military Police Office of Hongkong, which position, however, he did not like at all. Because of his poor health he got permission to come back to Tokyo with his Chinese wife, but being detained by some business at the last moment, he put his wife and her baggage on the ship and bid her good-by, telling her that he would follow her by the next boat.

The poor Chinese girl arrived in Tokyo in the midst of the bombing and came to the home of her husband's grandfather, who was a well-known businessman and who had a handsome house not far from where I lived then. She found the grandparents away in their country place and the big house taken care of by a younger uncle of her husband's. Her husband's father, an older son of the family, had died in World War I, serving in the Canadian army.

The uncle, aunt and their little daughter had no surplus food to feed the unexpected guest with, so naturally they were cold to their Chinese relative-in-law. The girl was starved but did not know where to get food. She could not get in touch with her husband, because her Japanese vocabulary was so limited. Her baggage, containing rice, soap and sugar, besides her clothes, had not arrived after four weeks' waiting.

She came to my house quite often after that. I wrote to her husband in Japanese, offered her a meal or two—which was all I could do for her in the way of food—and finally brought her to a boarding house run for the benefit of nisei boys and girls. Her baggage, when it finally arrived after our repeated inquiries at the Tokyo Station, was badly damaged and the best part of the contents stolen. Then, on the same night when my family was burnt out, her boarding house was destroyed. She and a few others continued to live in the corner of the half demolished office building nearby.

I took her to the Tokyo Military Police Headquarters, but could not obtain any help from them. She was dying to go back to Hongkong as she had heard nothing from or about her husband except to receive one money order from him. Then I thought of my friend in the East Asia Office. In trousers and tight-sleeved coat, and carrying a thick wadded hood to cover my head with, in case shells and chips of anti-aircraft bullets began to rain overhead, I picked my way through the streets clogged with broken tiles, rusted iron scraps, meshes of ripped electric wire and twisted carcasses of bicycles. No traffic service was operating in that part of the city, so I walked all the four miles. Nothing pained my heart more bitterly than the sight of the burnt bicycles. Against the mighty machine power of the B-29's, the raided people were unable to use even such an elementary machine as a bicycle. They had to flee, if they could, entirely on foot, carrying only what they could pile on their backs. So intensively destructive was the bombing that any area hit instantly turned into a wilderness tractable only by primitive beings.

At a few places I saw newly-made mounds with joss-sticks

burning or crumbled to ashes before them. I knew these were temporary graves.

The nearer I approached to the heart of the city, the rougher grew the sight. Bomb-gutted concrete or brick buildings lining the deserted thoroughfares, seemed as if they would topple down any moment with terrific rumbles, for these ghostly shapes seemed to hang in the air with fantastic semi-balance.

Just when I sighted in the distance the gaunt-looking government building to which I was going, the sirens began to hoot. There was nothing to do but walk on. The office building had already been half blown apart, and under the dark shadows of the mutilated walls the East Asia Office was barely operating. I found my friend in one of these dusky corners, but he simply shook his head. He said that he could have a certificate issued for the Chinese girl to leave Japan but that it would not help her much. When he was speaking, the sirens hooted again. Presently there was a distant rumbling noise, which gradually grew in volume, until it was amplified into massive booms of a hundred thunderclaps toppling upon each other in the cloud-muffled heavens. The mangled walls of the office building shook and groaned.

All was quiet after a while. We looked at each other's tight faces in the dimly lighted basement. I mumbled thanks to my friend and walked out of the office.

The western sky was black with high banks of smoke. Yokohama, the great seaport adjacent to Tokyo, with a population of half a million, had been wiped out in a single hour by three hundred B-29's tearing up the city with torrents of bombs, the biggest air attack so far experienced by the Japanese islands.

It is not with any personal resentment against the destruction caused by American planes that I am giving these detailed accounts of the bombing of the Tokyo area. It seems that human feelings cannot keep pace with the mighty progress of machine power. A friend of mine, who barely survived at Hiroshima, once said to me as if in a spirit of competition, "O, Tokyo and Yokohama are nothing in comparison with Hiroshima!" It seems that her remark somewhat represents the general sentiment of the world today. The big nations of the world, too absorbed in the horrible possibilities of atomic weapons, are apparently talking today as if nothing less than A-bombs counted much in the future warfare of mankind; as if bombing, so long as it did not go into atomic range, weighed lightly on their consideration and conscience. If I were a survivor of Hiroshima or Nagasaki, very probably I would have entertained the same sentiment. But having lived all through the protracted bombing of Tokyo, and witnessed with my own eyes the instantaneous destruction of Yokohama, and endured their multiple consequences, I cannot but feel differently. Not only I but countless other Japanese people, as well as many Koreans at present, know that bombing, even without involving atomic energy, can go a long way to undermine humanity. Am I wrong to say that the atomic weapons are dangerous not only for their destructive power, but also for their belittling effect on the fatality of other weapons which could irreparably harm the world while the world is too lost in the subject of atomic warfare?

6. The War Ends

In ruined Tokyo traffic and communication practically stopped. There was no way for my family to get in touch with our relatives and numerous friends who had lived in Tokyo the last time we had seen or heard about them, or who had gone into the country and left most of their possessions in their Tokyo homes. I walked miles and miles over the debris to see if their houses were still standing, but found practically nothing. Of the eleven families living in Tokyo and related either to my husband or myself, only two had their houses spared. There was about the same proportion in the cases of our friends, too. By and by I was informed that my cousins in Nagoya, Okayama and Osaka had been all burnt out. My eldest sister in Kobe, and my second sister in Wakayama, had escaped the fire.

"What is going to happen to us all?" we asked each other. Food conditions became worse than ever. Many food distributing offices having been burnt down, together with their precious stocks of supplies, we had now to walk a mile or more to get rice, potatoes, soy beans and bitter-tasting flour of acorn and sweet-potato vine. There was not a single wheelbarrow or even a baby's carriage, nor material to make any wheeled instrument with, in the neighborhood society to which my family newly belonged. Everything, no matter how heavy, had to be carried by one's own physical strength. I once carried home, in a group of similarly burdened women, 30 kg (67 lbs) of soy beans on my back, literally doubling up my body and crawling along like a beast of burden. No one on the street paid any attention to us, for such a sight was too common, and we housewives never minded the weight and our beastly appearance so long as it brought food to the family. I was sincerely and gratefully glad if, after standing two hours in a line, I could carry home a potful of bean-curd refuse or a pailful of watery gruel.

A few weeks after the destruction of our house, our youngest girl was taken into the country by her school. The night before she left, the family had a farewell party, in which we all prayed, sang hymns and wept, for we were not sure if we would see each other again. I took her to Ueno Station, spending hours on the way through air-raid warning and traffic interruptions, and finally put her on the train in care of her class teacher. I saw then that the big underground passageway adjacent to the station was already filled with refugees, some of them half-naked and covered with lice.

The family now suggested that the grandmother had better evacuate, too. Our only country relative, however, was my husband's distant cousin living 450 miles west of Tokyo. The old lady refused to go, saying that she would rather be bombed to death with her son and grandchildren. So she stayed on.

At this time, I had to make a trip into the mountains with the manuscripts of the English translation of some legal documents of Tokugawa Shogunate, entrusted to me by the Society for International Cultural Relations of Tokyo, for which I had been working for nearly ten years. This English translation of the detailed records of trials of the Yedo government, was started by Dr. John H. Wigmore of Northwestern University Law School of Chicago some 50 years earlier, when he taught at Keio University of Tokyo as a young professor of international law. It was resumed and nearly completed by the same Society by the request and cooperation of Dr. Wigmore himself. I was one of the translators, and when some manuscripts were ready for printing, I helped in the editing and proofreading. The war had cut off our communication with Dr. Wigmore and later we indirectly learned of his death.

During the bombing, the Society was completely occupied in sending away its precious collections of books and materials into places of safety. I thought I could not wait until the Evacuation Committee remembered the manuscripts in my charge. So toward the end of July, my young assistant and myself shouldered 15,000 typewritten pages between us, rode on a deck of an overflowing train past Karuizawa to Ueda, from whence we took a local electric railway into the mountain. After further climbing on foot, we deposited our precious charge in the bottom of a huge cave on a hillside, originally a granary, rented by the Society from a farmer. I made still another trip and brought up volumes of original texts and several hundred sheets of illustrative material.

I noticed then that the people of this mountain district were far more war-harassed than the citizens of Tokyo, probably because of the rumors that our military were demanding that

Nagano Prefecture be designated the last stronghold of Japan when the time came for the entire nation to perish.

When I came back from my last mountain trip, I was so tired that I felt I could not go on collecting food and feeding the family any more. The two children now left with us, were old enough to take care of themselves. Their grandmother, who was so overwhelmed by the rough circumstances of life, dozed day and night, and whenever awake, worried about the children not having enough to eat. In this stressed food situation, I thought we had better break up the family into smaller groups again, so that the children and the grandmother could see to the acquisition and regulation of their own food supplies. It was hard enough to control even one's own appetite in the face of ever-tightening food and fuel regulations. It was virtually impossible, however, for me to take charge of five people, including an always-hungry boy of seventeen, whose grandmother allowed him to eat whenever he liked, and thereby upset my food plans.

So my husband and I moved over to my aunt's house, which was at a comfortable walking distance from where the family now lived. Most miraculously this lovely house had been spared from fire, together with her son's old dilapidated house next to it. My aunt had gone into the mountain district of Shinano with her daughter-in-law and three grandchildren, and her son, left alone in Tokyo, lived with nine families of "burnt-outs" filling up the two houses and even the garage and the barn. My husband and I were given my aunt's living-room to use. Coming to live among this crowd of refugees, I felt more restful because I had now only my husband and myself to look after. Of course we were financially responsible for the children and their grandmother.

It took me some time to get acquainted with all the members of this big community. Besides my cousin, who was the owner of the houses, there were my two young cousins and their husbands, and some time later my brother-in-law joined us. The rest were people who had in some way or other been stranded there through the successive air-raids.

My two female cousins were Uncle Yasusaburo's daughters, both of whom had been married a few years previously and had lost practically all of their marriage trousseau. The older girl, after having been burnt out in one of the early raids on a snowy night, came over with her husband to live with her parents who, however, shortly afterward evacuated, leaving their house in charge of their two daughters and their husbands, the burnt-out couple and the younger one who had been living with the parents since her marriage.

On the same night that we were burnt out, their house received a shower of incendiary shells, their neighborhood being one of the hardest-bombed spots on that night. My older cousin was hit on the chest by a broken piece of shell. She thought she was dying. She fell on the ground and told her husband and sister and brother-in-law to leave her alone and fly for their lives, but her husband shouldered her and brought her out of the flames. When she was put down, and was assured that her feet could still support her on the earth, she was thrilled with joy. She later told me she had never before felt such intense joy of life. She added that a few of her familiar neighbors had perished on that night, including a well-known ex-diplomat, Viscount Y and his wife, both over eighty, who were seen groping through the curling sheets of smoke, hand in hand, but were never heard of again.

When I came to live with her in our cousin's house, her wound had practically healed although it still had to be bandaged. As soon as she could travel alone, she went into the country to join her parents and elder sister's family, leaving her husband, a bank clerk, in care of her younger sister and her husband, who was a synthetic oil specialist.

The non-related members of the community included a firm employee, a government official, a journalist, a major general, a barber, a street vendor, a poet, several wives and nearly a dozen children. There were four "evacuation widowers," or men living in the city after sending away their families into the country. These men depended on some other families within the community to prepare their meals. Each family grouped itself around a kitchen establishment of its own, which consisted of a mud oven or two, a pot or two, a knife and a few bowls and chopsticks, gathered in a bunch in any convenient corner of the compound. A common kitchen was impossible because now almost everyone had to feed himself with whatever food he could procure with his hard labor, heaps of money or ingenuity.

Shortly after my husband and I had settled in the new surroundings, the war came to an end with Japan's unconditional surrender to the Allied powers. At noon of August 15, 1945, all the tenants of the two Watanabe houses gathered around the radio receiver in the dining-room of the old, dilapidated main house, and heard the Emperor announce the surrender.

It was the first time the Japanese people had ever heard the Emperor's voice. Many of us had not been sure whether the Emperor *had* a human voice. He was divine, superhuman, merciful and mighty, so we had been told. But gentle and plaintive was the voice that came on the air. The preliminary announcement of "an important radio talk by the Emperor," who had never spoken in this way before, had already prepared the people. The audience was perfectly quiet. Some people sniffled and rubbed their eyes. "So after all," we said to ourselves. We had for some time been talking very privately among ourselves about this subject, but until the Emperor had spoken, we would not have formally and officially accepted the fact. The Imperial Edict for Surrender was simply a matter of form to us. Only we did not know whether we should be sad or glad.

We felt that the Emperor was really talking to his people through the radio. And hearing his human voice was as novel a sensation to us as our final and formal realization of the national surrender. We did not know then that his speech had been previously recorded and that the night before there had been a fierce fight over this record, a group of die-hard soldiers breaking into the Imperial Palace and demanding the destruction of the "shameful" Imperial speech. Nor did we know that there had been and still were desperate fights going on in various military units throughout the country, causing a great deal of killing, wounding and suicides.

The Emperor's tremulous voice flowed on, saying that with Russia now striking in the north, and atomic bombs in possession of the United States—two of them having already been used on Japan—no more resistance, however self-sacrificing on the part of the loyal Japanese people, was possible. Japan had but to surrender—surrender unconditionally in acceptance of the Declaration of Potsdam.

Very few of us in Tokyo knew then the details of the atomic bombing, so we did not know then what it really meant to Japan or to the world. All our newspapers at that time uniformly consisted of two pages and all printed the same government-issued war news. We tenants of the Watanabe houses took turns every morning in walking down half a mile to the news office, to bring home a bunch of papers and distribute them among the families. We did not expect much from these thin papers. Somehow I totally missed the news of Hiroshima in the *Asahi* which my husband and I were taking. I remember, however, reading just a few lines in the same paper, which said that a new kind of bomb, somewhat like, but not exactly the same as, the one dropped on Hiroshima, had just been dropped on Nagasaki and had caused some damage. This was all I came across in the way of immediate information regarding the A-bomb incidents. We housewives were so occupied with chopping wood and cooking meals and feeling hungry all the time that nothing less than the ending of the war would draw our serious attention. Nor did I hear the men around us talk much about the atomic bomb. Whatever happened in western Japan was not of much immediate concern to us in Tokyo, and our military government was most anxious to keep the people in ignorance.

So, not until the Emperor spoke did I know what atomic bombing was, and not until much later did I get any detailed information about Hiroshima and Nagasaki. Whatever else these two atomic bombs had done, I was glad that they had brought the war to a close. And I am sure all the rest of the people there felt the same way, at least for the moment, for none of them spoke against the use of them. Our militarist leaders had insisted on fighting out the war to the last man, dragging the entire Japanese people to destruction in their bloody wake. But now the majority of them were finally convinced of the total frustration of their medieval spiritualism before the power of modern science. They were no longer ashamed to admit their defeat, since nothing, not even the gods of Japan, could fight atomic weapons. And the Emperor personally declared this plain fact to his people.

The Japanese—militarists and the people alike—had once yearned for, and some of them honestly believed in, a timely intervention of divine powers who would descend on the desperate war situation and lead the Japanese nation to final victory. In the past national history of two millennia, all foreign invasions, including even the Mongolian menace of the 13th century which shook the entire known world of the time, had been, so we had been told, successfully repulsed by the aid of the divine winds always blowing adversely to the enemy and thus keeping the sacred islands of Japan forever intact against foreign conquest.

But in this terrible war of Japanese spiritualism versus modern science, their long-yearned for deus-ex-machina finally appeared in quite an unexpected direction of Heaven. He came out of the atomic bombs and spoke in the voice of the Emperor! Although I never believed in the divine protection of our islands, I had yearned for intervention of some sort to bring peace. So I could not, and still cannot, help but admit that the bombs with their horrors of gigantic proportion did bring or at least speed up, an end to our tragic war. I know some people disagree with me, and probably I am motivated by the limited experience of one who knew only the bombing of Tokyo. But still I sincerely persist in the view. I add, however, that although the first two A-bombs of mankind intervened for peace, this will never happen again.

"It means then that there is going to be no more bombing, doesn't it?" Mr. Yamanouchi, the barber, finally said amidst our pensive silence.

"That's true!" we all agreed and gradually brightened up. How good it was to realize that there was to be no more war, no more bombing, and no more fear of American soldiers landing on our coasts with the newest fighting machines. Now Japanese women and children wouldn't have to fight with bamboo spears!

"I hope," said Mr. Sato, the street vendor, in a fearful voice, "that they won't kill off the Japanese people when they come to occupy our country."

We did not know what the terms of surrender were going to be. In our past centuries of feudalism, surrender—in most cases—meant annihilation, or the most miserable form of slavery. So it was easier to fight it out to the last man, woman and child than to give in and be killed off in some way or other by the conqueror. It was simply through the motivation of this medieval code of war that the militarists had lured the nation to fight on to destruction.

Apparently, however, in the present scheme of the world, surrender did not mean annihilation. The Japanese people evidently were to survive their lost war. How to survive did not matter just then. To live was enough. I looked around and felt strange that I, as well as the rest of the people there, was still alive after all these horrors of war. Indeed, until a moment ago death was omnipotent and omnipresent, and to live was to go through an aggregation of a thousand hells. But the war was over at last! It did not matter how it ended.

We now noticed that the major general, who with his three children and a maid occupied the best upstairs room in the main house, had not come home since the night before last. I had known him only slightly. He was a tall, handsome, ruddy-faced man, a widower of about fifty, who occasionally quarrelled quite loudly with his children and particularly with the maid, a girl of the stodgy, straight-speaking, faithful servant type. His two daughters, fourteen and sixteen, and his son of eleven walked about in tattered clothes. Evidently these motherless children, left by themselves, had not saved a single thing from the fire and did not know how to take care of themselves in these strenuous circumstances. At any rate, when everyone was totally absorbed in the question of how to eat, what one wore or failed to wear did not seem to matter much. And truly we could do almost nothing for them. The general had a position in the War Ministry and was said to be discontented with the slowness of his promotion in comparison with some of his War College classmates. A few nights previously he had brought home a few bottles of liquor and had drunk all night with his army friends.

Two days after the national surrender, the report of the general's death was brought to us. We took it for granted that he had killed himself, since so many military men were reported to have committed suicide around that time. But later we were informed that he had died in a motorcar accident. The maid cried for him louder than anyone else, and tenderly looked after his children until some country relative came and took them away with him.

This major general, whom I came across just at the very end of the war, was the only Japanese military man I had ever personally known in my life.

Part Two

NATIONAL SURRENDER

∼∼∼∼∼∼∼∼∼∼∼∼∼∼∼∼∼∼∼∼∼∼∼∼∼∼∼∼∼∼∼∼∼

7. The Occupation Begins

During the short, anarchic interval between the Surrender and the Occupation, we at the Watanabe houses heard and passed on to each other wonderful stories of all sorts of supplies, up until now carefully stored for the uncertain future in the military controlled offices and firms, which were now being generously distributed among the employees. We were told that those offices that had stopped functioning with the close of war were sending their employees home with heaps of good things on their backs. We listened to these stories with endless envy. None of us had such luck, except perhaps my cousin's husband, a clerk in a big bank, who had brought home a goodly amount of clothing material.

Then we were told that a great deal of public goods which had been left over from the war, had been stolen and hidden away by whoever could lay hand on such "no-man's riches." Strings of motor-trucks, train-loads of army uniforms, warehouses of sugar, canned foods, leather, gasoline, became tremendous windfalls for various individuals, now that the military power had collapsed and lost control. At the time when a bad-smelling head of a fish or even a horse's still warm manure was eagerly picked off the street, a chunk of any kind of goods meant fabulous wealth.

The most vicious case of all concerned the diamonds surrendered to the government by the people during the war. They were supposedly handed over *en masse* to the Occupation authorities at the time of the seizure of national property, and had since been kept intact in their vault. But, as the Japanese people had just been informed, the glamorous stones have been inciting crimes and mystery stories ever since they were collected by various agencies on behalf of the government, and evidently at the time of national surrender were most active in their wicked wiles, though even in the hands of the Occupation they continued to be iniquitous.

But such luck or temptation came only to a limited group whose employers had had access to the inner mechanism of the "war guidance." Cases of downright robbery of public goods were rightly prosecuted later on by the Occupation authorities. The people in general had only slightly more appetizing foods, such as canned sardines and a bit of sugar and good rice, rationed just to celebrate the end of the war.

The Instrument of Surrender was to be signed on September 2, 1945, and followed by the immediate landing of the Allied forces in the Japanese islands. I never feared anything from the Occupation soldiers and felt strange at the frightful panic that spread over the people at the prospect of meeting the victors. Apparently my composure came from my past experiences with foreigners. I had been so well treated while in America that I had grown more fearless toward American people in general than toward most Japanese people. I felt sure I could talk with any of the American soldiers and make them understood as fellow humans. I also felt that they would be more thoughtful and courteous toward Japanese women than Japanese soldiers were. What was there, then, to fear?

But to most Japanese people, who had had very little personal contact with foreigners so far, it must have been terrifying to expect the arrival of tens of thousands of Allied soldiers whom they could not talk with. Particularly must it have been a horror to those people who knew something of what our occupation forces had done in China and the South Pacific. Evidently none of the refugee families of our community then knew about the war crimes of our armed forces, for none of us mentioned that subject on that occasion. We faced the occupation with a more settled state of mind than the majority of the Japanese people. The big size of our community probably gave us more assurance of safety. Mrs. Kawada, wife of the government railway official, brought home a cousin, an extremely pretty girl, whose husband was in Burma, and whose parents thought she would be safer in Mrs. Kawada's custody than in her own house. We all smilingly received the fair lady into our common charge.

Not only Mrs. Kawada's relatives but many other Japanese

parents and husbands sent away their daughters and wives to whatever places they could afford for hiding and safekeeping. Some young women, and quite old women too, solemnly cached a dose of poison—the most popular was cyankali—ready to swallow in an emergency.

Instructions came from many of the neighborhood-block offices, telling the women never to go out in mompé overalls because these solemn wartime clothes (baggy and ugly, the wearer often looking like a walking toad!) might be mistaken by the American soldiers for sleeping pajamas. They should be carefully and modestly dressed in kimono and obi, and should cover their feet with *tabi,* (white cotton socks which we were completely out of by this time), because showing one's body, particularly the feet, was considered most indecent in the Western countries.

After taking these precautions about women, the men with stern, worried looks on their faces—readied themselves to meet the Occupation forces.

My husband and I decided to stay on in the Watanabe community instead of going back to our children and their grandmother. Our youngest girl was still in the country in care of her school teachers. The older boy had come home the day after the surrender from his labor service at one of the naval supplies depots. Kazuko had just been graduated from the Tokyo Women's Medical College. There was no need to worry about them and their grandmother in connection with the Occupation. The food situation had not improved with the close of war, in fact it seemed to be getting worse, so I did not feel I could take on a household of six people just yet.

Our life in the community went on practically unchanged, but with increased amiability and cooperative spirit. Everyone wondered what was going to happen under the Occupation—to the country, to the Emperor, to the people's lives. But however varied were our political views and religious inclinations—there were rightists, leftists, middle-roaders, Buddhists, Christians, Shintoists, agnostics, atheists of all shades—and whatever our attitudes toward the Emperor worship, for or against its fall, we twenty-eight people of the community got along very nicely together. Differences of thought were unimportant when actual material life was so compelling.

There was no quarrelling about matters of social importance when all the twenty-eight men, women and children had to live under the same roofs, depending on a single hand-pumped well, three tolerably whole water pails and a good many leaky ones, two axes and a saw for hewing and chopping garden trees and furniture for firewood, a single wash-tub for the entire community—none of whose members, however, had much to change—a single baby carriage for carrying the rations of the eleven families home from the distributing offices, and a single bath-tub, which had to be filled with water every few days by relays of leaky pails from the distant well. This last activity was participated in by all the inmates, from the sad-looking poet to the chubby, grinning five-year-old boy, and beautifully performed because of their thorough training in this game in the air-defense drills.

Moreover, the social, economic and cultural levelling down of the Japanese people had been nearly completed by this time. No matter what our prewar social standings had been, we were now equally houseless, clothesless, hungry war refugees. Consequently the numerous families, living here with nothing but thin walls and frail partitioning screens between them, put up admirably with their lack of privacy, chiefly because they had nothing much to hide from each other in their uniformly deprived mode of life.

One thing in particular made us especially sympathetic with each other—our sense of having been miserably deceived by the military leaders. We had been told until the very moment of surrender that the fighting was still going on pretty hopefully, thanks to the superhuman bravery of the Imperial armed forces, and that even if the enemy landed on the Japanese homeland, they would be too few against the tens of millions of Japanese people, who definitely possessed "numerical superiority" over the invading enemy. Therefore we should not worry but trust and support the military to the last. How suddenly and how miserably all these bright promises and assurances collapsed!

Now the streets of Tokyo began to be filled with big American soldiers, gay and friendly. None of them clattered big shiny swords like Japanese army men, nor did they stamp their boots when they walked. In a word, they looked just as relaxed and unregimented as civilians. This was a very strange phenomenon to the Japanese observers. Many of the Americans rode in swift-moving chairs called "jeeps." The country roads were filled with their huge, handsome motor-trucks carrying abundant supplies of all kinds.

The sky buzzed with American planes. But how differently our old friends the B-29's now appeared from when they had raided the cities from high altitudes. Then they had looked so majestic and so ethereal, sparkling with silvery streams of exhaust gas trailing in their wake, while the citizens of Tokyo and many other towns looked up at them, standing on the very tip of their life-and-death stake. But now, stripped of all their awful glamor, they were plain machines, hard, metallic, shiny and mechanical just like any other flying machines!

And also how differently the Japanese cities looked to the Allied soldiers from the romantically advertised prewar Japan of lovely silks, gala-costumed geisha girls, and abundant souvenirs of pretty and inexpensive knicknacks. The restless GI's, wandering over what used to be the streets of Tokyo, peeped into the hovels built of iron scraps and carcasses of bicycles tied together in any possible way with bits of ripped wire, and asked the naked men or baggy mompé-trousered women within where they could find silk kimonos on sale, or if they could exchange a bar of chocolate for a picture card of Fuji-yama or a geisha girl.

Chocolate! The starved Japanese suddenly remembered their long-forgotten palatal joys.

"I will get some sweets," said Mrs. Kodama, the prettiest, youngest and bravest wife in our refugees' colony. She and her husband occupied the next room to mine. I knew the capable, energetic girl had saved a good store of kimonos and furniture. "What's the use," she grunted, "of having pretty kimonos when you have nothing to eat but acorn flour?" She dressed herself very attractively and went out with a good-sized bundle under her arm.

Her husband did not object, because he knew it was useless. His wife had grown totally unmanageable. Mr. Kodama was a good, gentle-hearted man. His chief fault was that he had been born in northern Kyushu, right in the midst of the hot-bed of our ultra-nationalism. He had been carried away by the surge of nationalist activity and during the early days of the war had been a prosperous press correspondent. He had traveled widely through Manchuria and the South Pacific countries, and then married his present wife, a handsome, rich, able and gifted girl. With the fall of the militarists he became jobless and financially broke. His wife thought she had been cheated and was very unhappy. But the people of the colony still liked him very much, because he made toys with bamboo sticks for the children and mended almost any kitchen utensils for the wives.

Mrs. Kodama was away for the whole day and came home beaming and flushed. "You should go downtown," she cried in great excitement, "and see what's happening, or else we will all be back numbers in this wonderful age of freedom and liberation!" She said that international trade had already been re-opened; that the rubble-filled boulevards were lined with stalls displaying anything and everything that had come out intact from the air-raids, ranging from gilt family altars to midget chopstick-stands; and that neatly dressed, heavy-pocketed American soldiers were threading through them in keen, friendly curiosity.

That evening Mrs. Kodama prepared a good dinner and was gay and good-humored toward her husband for the first time in some months.

"That's perfectly easy," said Mr. Sato, who used to draw a trundling stall piled with kitchen utensils and children's toys, and cater to housewives gossiping or airing their babies in the streets. In the latter days of the war he had nothing more to sell, so he became a factory hand. Then he was burnt out with his wife and two children and lost nearly all of his possessions including the trundle. But he had saved a good-sized suitcase, which he said would do well for his new start in trade.

He proposed to sell on commission for any members of our community. The refugees of the house had not much to offer for the business, but still there was a lovely cloisonné tray, a gold lacquer box, and heaps of silk pieces, all to be turned, if possible, into sweets, cotton socks, soap or towels. If exchange was unsuccessful, these might be sold for any amount of money he could get.

Mr. Sato had a few English lessons from volunteer teachers easily found in the community. He learned to count up to ten. Beyond that he said he could manage with his fingers and spirited "okays." American boys were very bright and clear-headed, he commented.

"But what is *otsuri* in English?" he asked me a few days later. A GI had given him a 10 yen bill and gone away without taking the change and he was feeling very uneasy. He wrote down "change" in Japanese letters in his notebook and felt well armed. "Next time I meet him, I will shout to him, 'Change!

Change! Your change!' " he said triumphantly. Then dropping his tone, he observed, "But the Occupation soldiers all look alike, don't they? Sometimes you get so bewildered because you get an impression that the same man comes to your stall over and over again a hundred times. They even wear their caps all alike—tilted on one side!"

"Don't they?" the listeners all agreed. The tilted caps of the Allied soldiers were a big curiosity to us. Peculiarly folded, always worn a bit tilted, they gave an easy, casual air, so different from the stiffness of Japanese soldiers who had had to wear their "sacred military cap" perfectly straight, or be punished. Once in a while some Occupation soldiers appeared with different caps, some looking like tam-o'-shanters and others wide-brimmed and feathered, but always a bit on one side. To Japanese men, wearing a headgear aslant was wellnigh a sacrilege.

Speaking of caps, Yasuhiko, my cousin's scientist husband, came home one evening without his "combat cap." He had been walking home, his mind deeply absorbed in some chemical problems he had to work out. All of a sudden a jeep passed by and something brushed his head. The next moment he was bareheaded and he could not find his cap anywhere.

His audience shrieked with laughter at the merry joke of the American soldier playing a "kite swooping off with the fried bean-curd." The serious-minded chemist did not well understand the humor of it. Moreover, the lost cap was the only headgear he had possessed and even an ugly combat cap like that could not be replaced in any way.

"I had better luck today," put in Mrs. Kodama. She was

walking along the Ginza, the biggest boulevard in Tokyo. Suddenly an Occupation soldier emptied a can of chocolate on the street. "It's all yours," he shouted and hurried away.

"How wonderful!" we all gasped.

People pounced on it, fighting with each other, and she was disgusted with these shameless beggars. Then she saw one of the candies lying at the tip of her shoe. She stepped on it lightly and just would not let it go, though she refused to stoop and pick it up like a woman of a conquered nation.

"What did you do?" we all asked.

"Well, anyway, I got it and ate it."

"How clever!" shouted Mr. Ono, the poet, with hearty laughter.

Even this high-browed man of leftish ideologies, hard to please and usually wearing a pale, sardonic face, was merry and sociable these days. He had been particularly elated over the liberation of political prisoners by the Occupation authorities soon after their landing in Japan. Among the liberated prisoners were many communists and sympathizers.

In this new age, even Communism could be freely talked about and followed. Of all the wonderful reforms the Occupation authorities started for the democratization of Japan, nothing was more impressive and spectacular to me, as well to many other Japanese, than the guarantee given for the freedom of political association and the consequent legal acknowledgment of Communism. At the same time it was announced that all the tyrannical laws of the old government were to be abolished. The rewriting of the National Constitution was to be effected according to truly democratic principles. This meant that the Emperor was no longer an infallible god, that there were no more titled and privileged classes, no more armed forces in the country, and that women were to have equal rights with men! Very soon a general election was to be held where women could both vote and be elected! We could not help but be happily and hopefully bewildered.

Fearful looks had long since disappeared from most Japanese men's faces, and their wives and daughters had been called back from their hiding. Some of the women dumped their "sacred poison" into the ditch, and boldly approached the Occupation men.

Allied soldiers began to appear in the street with Japanese girls, and their courteous manners toward their girl friends became a great novelty and wonder to the Japanese people. Crowds of women, as well as men, rushed to get employment in the Occupation offices. Girls put aside their ugly wartime costume and began to walk about in pretty kimonos or Western clothes brought back from country hide-outs.

"We can't sit idle," said Mr. Yamanouchi, the barber, and taking out his tools from the bundles of singed blankets deposited in the corner of his abode in the garage, he began to polish them. His wife offered to permanent-wave any of the women of the community for a very small charge, as she wanted to get back into practice. The Yamanouchis' professional eye quickly saw signs of a big boom coming to their business. They were the first to leave our community and get established in a barrack building of their own. Their business has since so thrived that they now manage a handsome beauty parlor.

Some other families gradually left our group and settled in other homes or migrated into provincial towns. Toward the end of that year my aunt came back from the country with her daughter-in-law and grandchildren. Now I had to think in earnest how to adjust myself and my family establishment to the new conditions.

8. Getting Started Again

Toward the end of 1945, prices began to rise alarmingly. My husband's salary and the small fees I was collecting here and there had become totally insufficient to finance our family economy. Every one with any knowledge of English was rushing to get liaison employment with the Occupation offices. I was greatly tempted. Just then I got a letter from a friend of mine, asking if I was interested in becoming a liaison secretary for the president of Tokyo Imperial University. Of course I was. But how could I appear in baggy, worn-out mompé overalls in any of the GHQ offices, to represent or accompany the president of the greatest university of Japan? I had saved some summer kimonos from the fire, but almost none for winter wear, and now that cold weather had set in, I had to pile on all the clothes I had. I wrote to my friend that I could not accept the position.

Some time later I was asked to teach English conversation to the employees of a chemical manufacturing company. For this position dress did not matter much, so I accepted the offer and went to the barrack-like office building of the factory once a week. Then I was occasionally asked to translate papers of various kinds into English. Since it was absolutely necessary now for me to earn as much money as possible, in order to keep the family alive against the currency inflation, my husband and I went back to live with the children and their grandmother, but on condition that I should be free from kitchen responsibility so that I could devote myself to earning money.

By this time the younger girl had come home from her school evacuation, and we now formed a family of seven people. Kazuko had just started her internship in a hospital. The older boy had one more year at Tokyo Imperial University, now called simply Tokyo University. The two younger children were still at high school. Their grandmother, now sixty-seven, had recovered some of her former vigor and was willing to manage the household.

The spring of 1946 was the worst time for our food situation. The government rations often got in arrears, and black market and free market prices were so exorbitant that we could not afford to get anything but a certain kind of seaweed, brownish-green strings, which looked and felt like strange-colored noodles. It filled our stomachs but was hard to digest. There was also wheat bran, from which we made thin gruel that was just a little more tasty than the calcic seaweed.

Occasionally I went back to see some of my old farmer friends, but their prices had also gone up, and I had no sewing-machine now on which to make shirts and trousers for them.

Unable to buy much, I picked up and brought home whatever the farmers had thrown away in the corners of their fields and found such collections good enough for my starving family. The children also took turns in these buying-out trips. They were beamingly triumphant if they brought home an armful of musty potatoes or withered turnips. Sometimes we had to spend a whole day at it, from early dawn to nightfall, just to carry home a load of sweet potatoes through the hellish traffic.

Finally we felt so weak that we could hardly stand or walk. The hardest trial for me was to walk three-quarters of a mile from the railway station to the office of the chemical factory once a week, to give my English lesson. I once fainted at the station and squatted—there was not a single bench to sit on— in the corner of the station, unable to walk for some hours. But no one paid attention to me, for everyone else was hungry and weak.

This was a time when people were more sincerely interested in what they had than in how they looked. Very often when I came across a neighbor on the street, carrying a bundle in my hand, the neighbor would look at my bundle with a keen, appraising gaze, but would seldom look at me. I must have acted the same way, for I often found myself lost in admiration of a full-stuffed rucksack on someone's back, or a big package tightly held in someone's hand, and wondering what nice things—rice, beef, chicken, eggs, apples—were stored inside it. I hardly noticed who the carrier was or how he looked. Goods were so rare, but dirty, tired people were everywhere, showing no individuality whatsoever.

By this time I had collected from my sympathetic relatives and friends enough clothes so that I could appear in public with a tolerable degree of respectability, at least from the Japanese standards of the time. The most serious problem was the rain outfit. I needed at least an umbrella if I was to get a regular job and go out every day. But my old silk umbrella, which I had miraculously saved from the fire, was irreparably torn and there were none to be bought. So I took the silk off the frame, then cut up a cotton kimono a cousin of mine had given me, sewed up the pieces into a circular shape and put it on the old frame. At any rate it renewed the umbrella to a serviceable degree. Later I helped several friends renew their umbrellas and in return for this service one of them gave me a silk water-proof coat to wear over my kimono. Now I could walk in the rain.

So I applied for a translator's position in the International Military Tribunal for the Far East, or the Major War Crimes Court. I was readily accepted, and began to work there in the summer of 1946.

About this time, abundant supplies of American foods were distributed to Japanese homes through the goodwill of the Occupation authorities. When big cans of delicious hams, bacon, sausage and butter were rationed at fabulously low prices, we were simply overwhelmed with joy and gratitude. But since the government stores of rice had evidently been exhausted, these rich fats were rationed in place of our staple foods, and we were lucky if we got a few thin slices of bread to go with them. For several meals we had nothing whatsoever but good, luscious sausages and bits of greens from our lean garden. We could not get even a handful of potatoes or beans. Apparently the American foods were distributed quite extensively, even in rural districts. I was told the story of a farmer's family puzzling over a huge can of butter. "What in the world can this be?" they said. "The safest way to eat a strange foreign food is to boil it in hot water!"

I was later told that these rich nourishing American foods were sent over to the Japanese at great sacrifices on the part of the Americans. They revived our vitality and rescued us from a desperate malnutrition problem.

With good foods came plenty of D.D.T., with which the health officers of the ward thoroughly sprayed our houses and gardens, not to speak of public buildings and traffic installations, while Occupation planes cleaned the air over us. In a sense it was the cleanest summer I ever experienced in my life. The burning of the city in the previous year evidently had destroyed many insects—such as ants and cicadas—living in the ground. But we had to wait for the D.D.T. to rid us of flies, mosquitos, fleas and lice. Together with these vicious bugs, the dragon-flies, butterflies and moths disappeared, too. The only ones I missed were the slender, red-bodied, golden-winged dragon-flies which used to ride on the gracious air of early autumn in large flocks, and which were so loved by Japanese children, poets and artists. Although some few flies and mosquitos remained, absolutely no other insects disturbed us that summer, at least where we lived. It was heavenly in that sense.

My war-wracked memory had another lift that summer when two Occupation officers unexpectedly called at my house to tell me that they had read "My Narrow Isle." I could hardly remember that I had once written a book by this title. My personal connections with America had been cut off by the Pacific War, and I was sure that all my personal friendships had been inevitably ended by it, too.

At the end of the previous year, however, I had received a heart-warming message from my best Wellesley classmate. When in the spring of 1946 the Education Commission visited Japan at the request of General MacArthur, I met Mrs. Horton, then President of Wellesley College, who brought greetings from my old classmates and some professors. But these were messages indirectly exchanged—since sending letters to and from Japan was, strictly speaking, illegal at that time. There is a great difference between talking with a friend, face to face, and hearing from one at second hand.

But this totally unexpected and surprising visit of two readers of my little autobiography, closely followed by the calls of a few others, suddenly revived in me my American consciousness —the feeling I had once had that I was a part of America.

Shortly after the visit of the two officers, one evening after dark a handsome U. S. army car stopped at my door and a gentleman jumped out of it. He said he was the husband of Doris Ferger, and handed his wife's letter to me. He had arrived in Tokyo the day before and had spent a great deal of that day hunting for my house. Doris Ferger? My mind was blank. All my American letters, pictures and books had gone, together with all the memories and associations attached to them. But after he had gone, suddenly the picture of a large-eyed, brunette girl returned to my memory, then her past letters telling me of her marriage, and one containing a picture of her baby daughter. The sixteen years' gap was instantly filled up! Some time later Doris herself came to Tokyo and to my house.

A few months later, my husband called my attention one morning to the picture of Hsieh Pin-hsin in a newspaper, with a big headline saying that the beloved Chinese poetess had come to Tokyo. I could hardly believe the news because during the war she had been reported to be dead. Later a journalist friend of mine had told me that the report was false, but still I had not been quite sure that she was still living. Suddenly my husband exclaimed, because the newspaper said that Hsieh Pin-hsin was looking for her old Japanese friend, Sumie Seo.

The following day, I think it was, the same journalist friend took me to see her at the Chinese Diplomatic Mission. There she was, a slim, dignified, middle-aged woman, war-worn, but her jet-black eyes just as lovely, peaceful and fearless as they looked when she was a young girl at Wellesley. She was with her husband and her youngest girl—she said she had left her two older children in Peking. Her husband, whom I knew at Wellesley as a shy, quiet, scholarly student visiting her, was now a high official in the Mission. Twenty years had elapsed since our happy American days. The first thing we said to each other was our sad regret that ten long years in the best period of our lives had been ruined by the war.

At the same time, however, I was thankful for the war in a way, because it brought right to my door these friends of long ago and far away, whom otherwise it would have been hardly possible for me to see again in my lifetime. Not only these two old Wellesley friends but many more came to Tokyo, some of them prewar residents of Tokyo returning to their changed old homes. Soon the Tokyo Wellesley Club had some twenty-five members representing the United States, Japan, China and India.

The most surprising fact was that we women of different countries, on suddenly meeting after a complete separation of nearly twenty years, had so much in common to talk about. When I was at Wellesley I always suffered from lack of conversational subjects with my college mates, because I felt I could not catch up with the American life around me. But now these twenty years had filled up that mental gap. In whatever parts of the world and in whatever cultural environments we had each been living, our experiences after our college days had been essentially similar—marriage, children, the responsibility of womanhood, and the war. Against these profound human events, our racial and cultural differences had long since been cast off. We now found ourselves close to each other without any of that conscious effort for international understanding and goodwill which we had learned in our young student days.

Around the autumn of 1946, I think it was, foreign mail was reopened for the Japanese people, and shortly after relief packages began to arrive from the United States. Many American friends, individually and through the Overseas Committee of Wellesley Alumnae Association, and later also through CARE, sent me packages of clothes, blankets, food, sewing thread, needles and soap, every bit of which was gratefully appreciated by my family, relatives and friends, for none of these precious things was yet obtainable in Tokyo, where people in general were still starved and shivering in rags. I felt that I had suddenly become a millionaire.

My mother-in-law, for the first time since my marriage, acknowledged the family advantages of having an American-educated daughter-in-law. She stopped complaining about my going out to work and putting aside household chores. I had become a greater economic asset to her than my husband, who during those post-war economic difficulties had to manage the school founded by his grandfather, which had been burnt down in one of the air-raids. She became entirely dependent on me and quite cooperative.

So I found the general tendencies of war-crushed, Occupied Japan quite congenial to me. I felt a kind of bitterness in realizing how long my American education had been kept idle, only to prove its usefulness after such hard, patient struggles on my part, and such wasteful, tragic occurrences on the part of the Japanese nation and of the world. At the same time I felt somewhat guilty to be finding myself comfortable amid such hosts of war-stricken, despairing people.

9. Peace Returns with Pots and Pans

What the inhabitants of Tokyo, men and women, old and young alike, hailed as the first sign of the return of peace was the clusters of stalls that arose at various traffic centers over the vast ruins of the city and displayed all sorts of homely commodities that the displaced, dispossessed people yearned for. Anyone wishing to buy anything had to resort to one of these markets. And evidently with a little capital anyone could rent a stall and a place and start business in one of these trading colonies, at least in the early days. Very soon the open-air markets grew in size and came under the strong-handed control of street bosses.

I felt an irresistible temptation to visit these booths. From the thickness of the crowds about them, and the frequency with which they were alluded to in our daily conversation, it was evident that they held the greatest interest for the Tokyo masses.

My favorite was the Shinjuku market, which I frequented more to see the things and crowds than to buy. The open-air sales went on in the scorching summer sun and biting winter wind, just because the people had to live on even in these hard times. Hundreds of booths, each smaller than the size of a bed, standing side by side in a double row lined either side of the bomb-gutted street, and through the narrow opening between the two files of stalls jostled the crowd.

People were clothed in any way, their dressing ingenuity being most noticeable in cold weather. Demobilized soldiers and repatriates from the south had nothing to wear but tattered, dirt-covered summer clothes. More lucky men walked in "dismantled" army uniforms, air-pilot's leather coats, Manchurian fur caps and Mongolian sheep skins. Some gentlemen had nothing but Parisian-style dinner jackets to wear.

Most women still wore ugly mompé trousers. When I came

across women in exquisite kimonos of heavy, solid, silk brocades, I could not but feel a heart-warming joy and gratitude for the survival of these works of art, although I knew that they too would be soon worn out, since they were the last resorts for the wearers who had used up or lost their more homely, durable cottons, woolens and pongees.

The Japanese, once such fussy dressers, had outgrown that weakness and did not care at all how they, or anyone else was dressed, so long as the clothes did not threaten to turn any moment into shreds and fall apart or get dirty. Dirty clothes were a problem because our soap smelled like dead fish and did not get anything clean and, when it was any good, cost like the rarest luxury in the world.

Of the multitude of people forever streaming by the rows of stalls, few actually bought anything at all. The jostling pedestrians passed on, just casting wistful and loving glances on the displays of goods, or sometimes slowing down their pace before some booths. They invariably joined the crowds gathered around certain booths where mending material was on sale, a woman energetically explaining how, with a hooked needle, you could sew up rips in shoes, slippers, bags and floor mats or to watch a man noisily pounding stoppers into damaged pots and pans and basins. At one time, booths selling iron plates for making molasses puff-balls, were big attractions, because many kilograms of brown sugar had been given out in place of rice and barley to the population of Tokyo. Countless households were wondering how best they could eat sugar three meals a day. Some time before, when they had got practically nothing but musty corn flour for several weeks on end, crowds used to collect around cracker-baking machines.

The people eagerly and delightedly watched these displays and demonstrations. Just a few, after long and ponderous deliberation on how best they could use the miserably small amount of money in their pockets, made their final choice from a hundred desirable alternatives and bought a flimsy kitchen knife or a stodgy-looking kettle made out of a queer alloy of metals once intended for munitions, paying a pile of paper money for it. Perhaps one out of a thousand was lucky enough to have heavy packs of money. These nouveaux riches practically monopolized all the buying that there was in this outdoor market of several hundred booths.

All the rest simply walked by, some tightening their mouths and others still gaping, admiring the sight of these homely commodities reappearing in the street scenes. The dawn of peace after the cataclysmic destruction shone far more beautifully on brand-new pots and pans and washing basins than pearly dewdrops, primroses and buttercups.

There was always a sensation and an expectant feeling among the booth-keepers, particularly vendors of curios and handy metal articles, when a group of American soldiers or a single GI with a Japanese girl came by, for these were ready buyers.

Sometimes the scene was rent with disturbances. "Who stole my peanuts?" I once heard a woman shriek in the midst of the crowd. Evidently her big box of peanuts, costing thousands of yen, and placed right in the middle of her booth, had been stolen during the few seconds while she was trying to get her

100 yen bill broken into change by a neighbor. She began to run back and forth, trying to find the thief in the crowd. Failing, she leaned on her stall and began to cry. She said she was a repatriate from Manchuria, with three children and an invalid husband, living under the floor of a Buddhist temple. Anyone robbing a poor woman like her would surely be punished by the gods, she sobbingly declared. The neighboring booth-keepers were all sorry for her, but robbery was too common a phenomenon in this place or anywhere in the post-war cities of Japan to raise any sensation. "What a shame!" the neighbors said and went on with their business and the guarding of their commodities and purses.

"You thief!" a man once yelled into my face and stupefied me. A tiny, ragged boy ducked by me but was caught the next moment by the pursuer, who held his victim by the neck, pulled out of his pants' pocket a handful of toffee, slapped him on the cheek and let go. "Wait a minute," a young woman cried. "I'll buy the candies for the boy." She held out a 100-yen bill to the toffee-man, who, still in a disgruntled mood, offered the candies back to the boy. "Never mind," the tiny urchin said, looking up at the gruff man and the kind girl with his chubby, dirt-covered, wet-nosed face. "It was a punishment for my clumsiness. I'll do it better next time. So you wait!" And the little rogue darted away into the midst of the crowd.

The eating stalls, which were grouped apart from the others, presented a somewhat different scene. Here were far more consumers than lookers-on, for the delicious smells of roasted pork, fried shrimps and broiled fish, mingled with strong odors of cooking onions, soy-bean sauce and whale oil were imperative. The reed-screened booths stood in countless rows while some vendors—mostly women with little children—who could not afford to hire a booth, simply spread their piles of steamed sweet potatoes and bean-jam dumplings on up-turned wooden boxes, and squatted before them. The market was jammed with hungry eaters, for the rationed food was scanty and limited in variety, and many people had no kitchen whatsoever to cook their meals in.

With a mixture of fear, shyness and self-pity, I walked through the jostling throng, and was sometimes tempted to a stall of broiled herring or cuttle-fish, piping and shimmering hot. One big booth was particularly crowded, people standing in a long queue to get a big bowl of chicken broth at a surprisingly low price. It was said that the food served here was particularly delicious because it was made of left-overs from some quarters of the Occupation army. I noticed a number of little children darting about and holding out their hands to the eaters, and some booth-keepers driving them off with bamboo sticks. A few people, who felt extremely uneasy at the sight, gave them some left-overs.

Besides the inviting calls of the vendors, the place was filled with noises of all kinds. Once I was startled by a heavy dropping sound, followed by strange cackling noises. Just a few yards away, a pretty, pale-faced young girl had let fall a big bowl of noodles, and two rag-covered figures had instantly pounced on it and were fighting over the spilled food. The two figures were both lean and short, one hunch-backed and the other limping. Their dingy hairiness identified them as grown-up men, but their flapping movements and queer utterances made them look more like two sickly roosters. With animal greed and shamelessness they clawed up the noodles from the ground and gobbled them with a loud lapping sound.

I stood completely awe-struck. "Hey, you thief, don't steal my cigarette end!" a shrill voice suddenly screamed at my side, and I saw a tiny boy of six or so snatch a cigarette butt from the man who had just picked it up.

"Did you drop it?" the man asked in surprise. "You are awfully young to smoke."

"I don't care for smoking myself," the child spoke like a man. "Don't you know I pick up cigarette butts and sell them to cigarette makers? This is our territory. No one outside our union is allowed to pick up a cigarette in this area."

"Hm. I didn't know that. I have been repatriated only recently," the man in the patched, khaki-colored summer coat said apologetically.

"So you are a poor repatriate without a job, eh?" the boy assumed a patronizing air. "If you want to pick cigarettes here, you'll have to ask our boss and join the union. It's a good job—wonderful on Sundays when Allied soldiers are out. Only you have to be awfully quick. See that woman ready to throw her cigarette?" And the boy dashed away, dangling his pick-bag by his side.

Night scenes at these street markets were sad, and more dominated by women. I did not enjoy visiting them at night, but I had to walk through them sometimes when I went out on business. The stalls, particularly the eating stalls, were crowded with young girls, thickly painted, and wearing short skirts and scanty blouses, or trousers tucked up high. Evidently eating stalls kept open far into the night, though other vendors had to close their booths when the pedestrian traffic thinned out. I wondered where these street vendors spent the night, or if they had a home to go back to. I noticed that there were more women than men in charge of these stalls late at night, often with their children by their side.

10. Drifting Human Wreckage

The buoyant anticipation with which we faced the national surrender and the democratic reforms launched by the Occupation gradually sobered down when we came to realize the vastness and complexity of the war's consequences. In fact, these aftermaths often seemed to baffle the rehabilitation efforts of our national government, even with the generous assistance of the Occupation authorities.

The question of food was so imperative that it took precedence even over the problem of housing for displaced people. Spread over the ruins of Tokyo, millions of people lived any which way. Few had proper houses, and the majority huddled in tumbling down ruins left from the fires, or in shacks built from whatever war debris could be picked up on the spot. Several families often shared a single room. Yet these people were envied, because there were tens of thousands who had no homes except the basements of bombed buildings, underground passageways, slopes of river banks, under bridges, temple yards, and under the floors of temple halls and any other places that offered some degree of shelter from Tokyo's damp, treacherous weather.

Moreover, the slowly recovering traffic of the city was instantly thrown out of gear by a thunderstorm or a snowfall, when travelers were left to shiver in mud and water for hours, and often overnight. I joined such crowds of the "open air population" several times, and came to realize thoroughly the meaning of the Chinese word, *Liu-min,* or "human wreckage." The recent wars have left the world inundated with enormous masses of drifting human wreckage.

Once my husband and I had to make a trip into the country. I think it was in the early autumn of 1946. On our way home, when we were nearing Tokyo, raindrops began to hit aslant the cracked glass-panes of the train windows. We looked at each other in utter despondence. At that time we feared and hated rain more than almost anything else, because our flimsy rain outfits, so laboriously and expensively collected and repaired, would be instantly ruined in a heavy shower. It was far more economical and much safer against catching cold if one hugged the precious umbrella, shoes, clothes and all in one's arms and ran any distance home as fast as one could.

When the train pulled into the terminal, the rain was pouring down in torrents. In the darkness of the descending night, the people stood in the unlighted station hall, mute, sad, shivering. The wind blew sprays and gusts of cold rain through the doorless entrance and countless cracks of the dilapidated building. Just a few small lamps were lighted by a local electric circuit in the dark, spacious interior. It fell dimly on the people's drawn, perplexed faces which shone in intense delineation whenever the lightning flashed across them.

Some one said, "Let us move into the underground. It must be warmer and drier there," and a stream of people began to move toward it. My husband and I were caught and pushed on in the stream. After having been knocked about for some time, we found ourselves stranded in some unknown part of the big, concrete-walled subterranean highway, which leads from Ueno Central Station to the underground tramway and then on to another electric railway terminus.

The passage had been already quite filled before the stream of people began to flow into it. The regular inmates had been driven back by the rain earlier that day to their straw and newspaper beds.

"Hey, get out. Don't come into our roped area!" a gruff voice called out of the obscure depth of the vault. Many heads popped up and many bodies squirmed about. The place was stuffy with peculiar, rancid odors. A few oil lamps hung on the wall.

Some of the streaming men pleaded, explaining their plight.

"We'll have to ask our boss," said another voice, just as gruff.

After some noisy murmurings that echoed through the vaulted walls, a rough, imperious call came. "Let them in just for tonight, gratis."

Cordial relations were soon established, and the original inmates made room for the intruders. Indeed, we were intruders, for the proper inhabitants of the cave had long established their right of domicile. The earliest colonists had settled immediately after they had been burnt out in one or another of the air-raids. Each individual or family had acquired by usage the right to occupy a certain regular spot on the concrete floor of the covered passage. Each later comer had to pay "privilege money"—which had now gone up to 1,000 yen— to the boss of the group. The entire passageway was divided into several sub-territories and each group had a boss, who was subordinate to the Big Boss. The origin of the Big Boss was obscure, except that he was one of the early settlers with organizing and governing ability. The place was run on a pattern of patriarchal absolutism with laws and means of self-defense of its own, like the pattern reproduced everywhere in the disintegrated social life of postwar Japan.

The boss's command instantly settled the question and the entire cave played open house that night as graciously as it could manage. The hosts and guests very soon got into a social mood. I was all ears.

"Are you a burnt-out or a repatriate?" one of the temporary refugees asked one of the inmates. This was invariably the first question one drifter asked of another.

"I am a repatriate from Manchuria," a man in a hoarse voice answered.

"Repatriates are even worse than burnt-outs, aren't they?" said another temporary refugee, with a sympathetic look at the hoarse man and his equally hoarse, stupefied-looking wife, sitting together on a tattered piece of straw mat with a single dirty blanket for a cover.

"I suppose so," the repatriate sadly responded. "My wife and I worked hard for twenty-three years in Hsin-king. We had a good business and a happy home there, but see what it has all amounted to."

Surrounded by a new group of people that evening and asked many sympathetic questions, the man began to tell his story. He and his family had followed the stream of fleeing Japanese from all the Japanese outposts on the continent, that finally collected into a big group of panic-stricken, hunger-harassed ex-emigrants, hurrying home now that Imperial Japan had collapsed in rubble and rubbish. His son was later recalled to Hsinking and they had not heard of him since. They took trains whenever possible but had to walk a long way through the wilderness of South Manchuria, famished and exhausted, where Manchu farmers, showing bags of *kaoliang,* offered to exchange them for Japanese children.

They were held up in North Korea and passed the winter there, in a refugees' camp in a country town. One day his daughter-in-law became a little queer, and suddenly disappeared with her two children. She was never found. The man and his wife marched on, tattered and barefooted. Staggering and propping each other up, they climbed many hills in scorching heat and waded many rivers in torrents of rain. Finally they crossed the 38th Parallel into South Korea, where the refugees were given food and medical care by the Allied army, and relayed on to the homeland of Japan.

"People fell by the hundred on the way. I saw little children covered with worms before they were really dead," he said. "I looked at every one of these children, wondering if it could be either of my lost little ones."

"Did we ever dream," put in one of the listeners, "of such a miserable end for our so-much propagandized, so-much glorified Manchurian projects? The government urged us with many rosy promises to settle on the Continent. The military and the government men were the first to hustle their families home when they knew they were losing the war, never minding the emigrants trapped in the terrible situation. And now see how the repatriates are treated at home."

"Who can tell me," a woman's painful voice asked, "what time it is now?"

No one around had such a thing as a working watch. That it had already been dark an hour in the outside world, and that it must be still raining and thundering, was all the information that the people could give her.

"I am a burnt-out," she said. She had lost track of her husband and boy in an air-raid and became stranded there with her daughter a year ago.

"Where is your daughter?" some neighbors asked.

"She has gone out to sell evening papers. She is only twelve but she insists on working while I rest until I am cured of this rheumatism."

"Rheumatism won't get cured here, will it?"

"No. But whatever has become of my girl?" She began to sob.

The tired, cold, hungry people now got ready to pass the night in the vault. They spread on the concrete floor newspapers, handkerchiefs, towels and whatever else they could find. Fortunately almost every one of the stranded travelers had a big bundle or two. These served for pillows to lean on. Gradually the crowd settled down and became quiet.

My husband and I squatted, sharing a single sheet of newspaper, and leaned on the rucksack each of us carried. Through my wet socks and trousers I keenly felt the cold and dampness of the concrete floor. So I kept moving and wriggling, trying hard not to poke into any of the huddled people around me.

"Leave me alone. That's none of your business!" A woman's sharp voice suddenly arose some distance away.

"The rainstorm has ruined my night's business and I haven't eaten a single thing today. I need money terribly, so I offer my services to any one of you here."

Vulgar laughter and teasing remarks were heard.

"I don't mind," the girl protested tauntingly. "I don't mind at all lying with a man in public, even right here before everybody, but men are all cowards."

"Hurray, go ahead!" some one cheered. "That would be a wonderful show for us. *He, he, he!*"

With a sense of painful shock, I huddled on the pile of sweet potatoes, beans and stone-leek with which my country friend had stuffed my rucksack. Then I remembered that I must not crush the silk brocade kimono wrapped in many sheets of newspaper and carefully deposited in the midst of the precious food stuff.

· 96 ·

This kimono was also a gift from my friend. It originally belonged to a friend of one of her daughters, who had sent a chest of kimonos from Tokyo to the country for safekeeping during the war. After the war, my friend had tried every possible means of tracing the whereabouts of the girl and her family, but had totally failed, and concluded that they must have been all wiped out in the flames. She now thought that the best way of fulfilling her responsibility was to distribute the contents of the chest to burnt-out people, so that those lovely kimonos might warm the hearts and bodies of the war-sufferers and thereby earn sweet prayers from them for the departed soul of the unfortunate maiden. Before she gave one to me, she put it on her family altar and recited the supplicatory prayers to the All-saving Amida Buddha.

Her supplications now kept ringing in my ears and the lovely purple brocade in my possession reminded me of the halo of Buddhist Heaven. I looked about me at the huddled lumps of human bodies, most of them completely still now. The small oil lamps shone just distinctly enough to show me objects in the shapes of rags and the color of dirt, stretching out into blurred obscurity at both ends of the tunnel.

Occasionally I thought I heard a faint groaning sound somewhere, but I could not tell whether it was the suppressed utterance of my pained heart, or of someone else's, or of all the sufferers there. Everything in my mind and in the outside world seemed to recede from me, leaving me in the cold, damp, gray void. The pungent, never pleasant smell that rose out of the stone-leek I carried in my bag evidently worked a strangely soothing, medicinal effect on me in the stuffy, rank air of the vault. I must have dozed.

I felt my husband stir, and then I heard "um-m-m-m," a distinct sound of pain. "The city circuit line has started working," some one shouted and the news was relayed on. When my husband and I got up to go, I noticed a group of people peering over something. A girl lay on a mat in great pain. She was so emaciated that, but for her black, dirt-covered abundant hair, she would have been taken for an old shrivelled-up woman. She had a burn on her face. By her side sat an elderly woman, probably her mother, leaning against a rattan wallet, which was apparently the only possession now left to the poor burnt-out mother and daughter. I mutely placed a 10 yen bill on the pile of paper money that some of the crowd had piled by the girl's side.

Then I remembered the woman with rheumatism who had been worrying last night over her child who had not returned home to the vault. Looking for her, I was overjoyed when I found her with a little girl asleep in her arms. The brave child, after selling her evening papers in that thunderstorm, had found her way back to her sick mother. With my husband's consent, I took out the two seaweed-covered rice balls I had left in my rucksack and placed them before the woman. Our country friend had given us a box of rice balls to eat on the train, and they were so good that we had decided to save some, and take them home to our family. But we thought that the ailing woman and her little girl needed the food we had, far more than our family did, so it was really an offering from our entire family. Tears welled in my eyes and suddenly there rang in my ears a voice saying, "It is more blessed to give than to receive!" Among the hungry and displaced, how intensely and how overwhelmingly true was that most elemental of earthly blessings!

It was bright dawn in the outside world, and just as we were leaving the vault, several little boys ran past us, each with a sizable box under his arm. "Grown-ups are all cheats. Don't trust them," one of them was saying to the rest. They were boot-blacks hustling to their breakfast stalls.

I soon discovered that our hosts of human wreckage included vast numbers of young women, drifting about and clogging junctions of the city. Even in the broad daylight they approached the wandering men. The more aggressive, hard-working ones invaded tramcars, movie houses and any other place, except perhaps, private homes.

After nightfall they busied themselves in dead earnest. "Short time?" "All night?" they would call out in their peculiar Japanese-English. Bargains were mostly "short time," quickly made and fulfilled outdoors under the cover of night in the black shadows of the war debris. A roof over the head was too high a price to pay for average transactions.

The current word to designate this type of street women was "pun-pun." All sorts of etymological speculations were being made about its origin, but none was convincing enough. All we knew was that it was a word of wide postwar use and was thought, at least by the Japanese people, to have originated in the Occupation army.

These girls were so omnipresent at one time that all of the men of my family had many experiences with their seductive whispering, "Brother, keep company with me." My shabbily dressed husband laughingly reported to me one day that he had been called to by a girl, but that when she saw his homemade, patched-up cotton bag, which he had been in the habit of carrying ever since his leather brief-case had been burnt in the air-raid, the girl readily let him go. We then called the miserable bag "the pun-pun bouncer," and valued it greatly. My younger boy once looked very handsome and "war-prosperous" in a beautiful suit sent to me in one of the gift packages from America. Shortly I had to take the suit away from him and put him back in his old clothes. Later, at the request of a friend of mine, I passed it on to her son, but all the time I felt as though it might weave deadly temptations around that innocent young boy.

One day, in a jostling street crowd, I saw people making way for a beautifully painted, handsome woman, who was striding along in gray-colored trousers. I overheard someone say, "Madam Omasa." I knew then that she was the president of the sorority of street girls of that locality. Her name had long been familiar to me, for people at that time talked about pun-pun girls and their method of business management as commonly as their food and housing questions.

The abolition of licensed prostitution, which was one of the very first reformative measures of the Occupation-controlled government, did away with this Japanese institution of many centuries. But the material and mental bankruptcy of the war-crushed nation pressed hosts of starved and filth-covered girls to stand, of their own will or necessity, on bomb-gutted, rubble-clotted street corners. In this new form of prostitution, there were no avaricious employers, as in the old system, to exploit the girls to the last degree of their physical capacity. Nor was there the serious question of postwar taxes to affect their business, because it was not licensed. The girls' earnings were all their own. Evidently this advantage drew many women into the profession, and indeed, they were far better off—or at least better *fed,* so we were told—than the malnutritioned masses.

On the other hand, these girls were entirely unprotected by law, unlike the old "birds in the cage" who were altogether too well watched over by their employers in cooperation with the police authorities. Necessity taught them to organize, but the transportation difficulties kept them in small local units. Older, capable, experienced girls became leaders, and around them gathered several scores of girls, mostly teen-agers, and thus a unit grew. They set up their headquarters, elected their president, directors and other officers and had a council and a general assembly. They collected dues and laid by common funds.

They knit themselves tightly together against all outside enemies, negotiated with other local units, and drew up boundaries for the sphere of interest of each group which they called the "roped territory," a term long in use in the feudal laws of Japan. Each group was to engage in trade strictly within its roped territory, and any case of trespassing was punished in any way possible by the collective force of the women of the offended unit.

The president and directors were awarded the title of *neisan*, or "elder sisters." They formed a compact matriarchal body for the rest of the members and most efficiently helped them out of any difficulty—financial, social or physical. They gave advice to the younger girls on how best to avoid the physical consequences of their profession. They sent financial aids and sentimental encouragement when any of their members were arrested and sent to the hospital by the police. In the social gossip of postwar Tokyo some of these "elder sisters" became famous figures.

Theirs was a complete self-government, most efficiently organized for self-defense. Women in this outcast profession had learned, out of sheer necessity, to defend their interests by their organized strength, which was derived from their absolute obedience to the matriarchal powers of the Board of Directors, their closely-knit mutual aid system, and their compact unity against outside hostility. Any violation of the agreements within the organization was as severely and as brutally retaliated as an intrusion from another group.

In the financing of their common funds and even in the punishment of a law-breaker, these women were perfectly self-sufficient. If there was any masculine element connected with their organization except as sources of their incomes, it was the vicious parasites who sometimes fastened on some of the girls and sucked into them. But even these were bravely fought down and eventually cast off as common enemies by the girls in close cooperation. Of necessity these were hard-headed, strong-fisted, perfectly competent business women. Business was business to them. A pale, flabby-limbed teen-ager, picking up a "brother," would lie down on any conveniently sheltered spot, often an abandoned air-raid shelter by the roadside, and calmly wait, her eyes looking so perfectly innocent and unconcerned that often the client was taken aback.

"How and when are we to recover some of our old decency and comfort?" the Japanese people asked themselves, without expecting answers. Whether properly housed or not, they all felt themselves totally insecure in the constant ups and downs of postwar Japanese life. In that sense, they were all helplessly drifting and could not rise much above the rudimentary questions of food, clothing, shelter and sexual interest. The way to rehabilitation seemed hopeless and endlessly long.

Part Three

THE WAR CRIMES TRIALS

~·~

11. The International Military Tribunal

When I began to work in the International Military Tribunal for the Far East, or the Major War Crimes Court, in the summer of 1946, the prosecution had been going on for several weeks. I chose the War Crimes Court because I had been told that the Japanese employees there were better paid than in regular GHQ offices. I had no particular interest in the trials at that time. I was assigned to the Defense Section of the Tribunal, simply because the Prosecution had already been well started with efficient staffs in full operation, while the Defense was just organizing its language division and taking in many translators. I had no choice of my own regarding what section I should like to work in, indeed until actually placed, I did not know that there were, besides the Tribunal proper, distinct prosecution and defense establishments in the Court, each with an enormous staff, and various divisions and subdivisions. But later I found that, of all the offices of the Occupation connections, the Defense Section of the Major War Crimes Court was the most pleasant place for Japanese employees to work in.

My monthly salary for 40 hours a week was 1,800 yen, paid by the Japanese government. Until the previous year I had 50 yen a month for working two days a week at the Society for International Cultural Relations. My new salary was more than fourteen times the old, but currency inflation was so rapid that this big sum soon became totally deficient. It had to be readjusted many times, and in two years was raised to ten times the initial sum. The 18,000 yen which I came to earn was equivalent to $50 a month at the official exchange rate, and about 25% was taken away for income tax.

The War Crimes Court sat in the former War Ministry building. I daily commuted from my house by taking a suburban electric line to Shinjuku junction, then the Central Government Railway to five stations beyond, then a five minutes' walk. This was a thirty minute trip, but usually it took me more than an hour and quite often two hours, because I had to let many crowded cars go by before I finally succeeded in hanging onto one. All the Japanese workers at the Court had the same traffic problem.

The traffic in Tokyo was really hellish. It had got this way in the latter days of the war, and was one of the slowest phases of postwar city life to recover. People had crowded into the suburban areas of Tokyo and neighboring towns, and now commuted to the gradually recovering and throbbing centre of the city for business, amusement, black market and what not. Every car was packed to its last possible capacity. Each rider simply wedged himself in with his own bodily strength or by someone else's assistance, until the passengers, like canned sardines, took whatever crooked shapes they were pressed into. The pliability of the human body under high pressure was quite amazing. We felt each other's existence simply in terms of human bones— not dead white bones, but hard shoulder-blades and elbows drilling into tender and sensitive ribs and entwining with each other. The least jerk of the car was enough to cause the bulging window-panes to crack and send an over-balanced rider off.

Traffic casualities were so common that I, who did not see any actual dead bodies during the war when tens of thousands of people perished in the bombing, came upon them twice in short succession soon after I had started commuting to the city centre. After each car-ride I heartily congratulated myself on my safe arrival, and at the same time found my clothes ripped and stained with grimy handmarks. I had not much clothing to change, and soap was still a costly luxury. The hectic traffic, more than anything else, tried our postwar patience.

It took me several months to get acquainted with the detail of the complex composition of the War Crimes Court, and the plans of the War Ministry building where the court functioned. I was a member of the translators' pool in the Defense Section. I sat all day at my desk in the big office room on the ground floor of the building and translated Japanese documents into English. Each defendant had an American and a Japanese defense counsel who had an office of their own on the second floor of the Defense wing, with their own clerical and language staff. I had no direct business with these people. The Tribunal consisted of judges from eleven Allied nations, with its big clerical staff, and guarded by a large body of the military police. The Prosecution also represented the eleven Allied countries and had extensive investigation and translation organs. These were located far from my office, though within the same building.

We translators were given spectators' tickets in turn. But I went into the court room only once all through the time I worked there. The court room presented a spectacular and impressive scene. The decoration of the Allied flags over the highly raised bench where the judges sat, facing the twenty-five—originally twenty-eight—figures of men who were once commanding and powerful figures in the eyes of the Japanese people; the large prosecution and defense group facing each other on either side of the judges; the electrical appliances controlling the sound and light effects; the various languages, besides Japanese and English, which were translated through ear-phones—all conspired to produce a magnificent spectacle.

Every day the Japanese people formed a long queue at the Foreign Office to get spectators' tickets, and another long queue at the court entrance to get good seats.

I had very little chance to come to know personally any of the defendants and their families. I could look up from my office to the barred windows behind which the prisoners rested while out of the court room. Occasionally I came across the closed bus which took them back and forth between the court and Sugamo Prison. Once I acted as interpreter for the lovely wife of General Hashimoto and went with her to see Colonel Kenworthy, Chief of the Military Police Guards of the Tribunal and the Prison and the beloved guardian of the national prisoners and their families.

The trials of our major war crime suspects were staged at the site of our former War Ministry and Army General Staff. This fact seemed to deepen the sense of the tragedy of our fallen militarism. Some people among my colleagues at the court had worked as clerks in the same building during the war, and knew exciting stories about the last days of the War Ministry, although they were disinclined to refer to them too frequently. For me the place had no association whatsoever. Only the sight of the perfectly preserved buildings, standing by themselves on the hilltop in the midst of vast wastelands of war debris, told me the amazing accuracy of American bombing. From more than 10,000 meter altitudes, the American bombers had clearly followed the boundary walls of the War Ministry grounds and wiped out everything outside them, including the Shinto Shrine of the War-God nearby. But they had left intact, out of sheer respect, our National Shrine of Dead Soldiers standing just across the moat from the War Ministry hill.

Daily I walked up and down the hill, looking on the ruins of what used to be some of the best residential sections of Tokyo. On one side, checkered with patches of potatoes and wheat growing over what had been exquisite ornamental gardens, stood countless numbers of tall chimneys, each rising abruptly by itself from the ground. These were the only remnants of the wealthy, modern homes that had been there. Looking on this scenery from a distance, you had an illusion of beholding some Mohammedan city with countless minarets rising to the sky. Far in the distance, silhouetted against the sky, you could see the tops of modern apartment buildings in the downtown area. The sight of the minarets in the foreground and the square buildings in the back was completely bewildering, and made you wonder where in the world you had strayed. Certainly there was nothing Japanese in the view.

If you looked at the neighboring scenery more closely, you noticed skeletons of garden trees standing in as stark loneliness as the ruined chimneys. The biggest tree skeleton in this neighborhood was that of the camphor tree in the precincts of the Shrine of the War-God, said to have been the second oldest tree of its kind in all Tokyo. Standing as it did on the abruptly rising front of the War Ministry hill, no one coming into this locality could miss it. Once a superabundance of glossy green foliage nesting flocks of birds, but now a silvery, sharp-pronged object, gigantic, monstrous, heart-rending, it stretched its symmetrically forked, totally denuded boughs high up into the sky. It had stood there for five centuries as one of the most sacred trees in the town of Yedo. The bent-backed, modest-mannered people of the Tokugawa Age looked up to its glorious stature with wonder and adoration, as pictured by one of the 19th century artists of the Hiroshige School.

Lost houses can be rebuilt, but the death of old trees is never to be requited. So I cried with joy when I discovered that the gingko trees over the ruins of Tokyo were not quite dead. With the return of spring, tiny shoots were oozing out of nearly every one of their charred, stubby trunks, ready to burst forth into soft, bluish-green, fan-shaped foliage. Evidently gingko trees are salamanders to have endured through those hurricanes of fires. Now their mutilated yet vigorously reviving figures, marking many a site of ancient worship, served the aching hearts of the citizens of Tokyo as dear landmarks for the map of the lost city.

I worked in the War Crimes Court for two years and five months. During all that time the surrounding scenery of war devastation remained unchanged except for the further overgrowth of big, fat weeds. The War Ministry hilltop alone was busy and alive. The old buildings were cleaned and beautifully furnished and housed hundreds of offices. The cherry trees on the hillside bloomed twice, each time making a flowery arch for the prisoners to pass under on their way to and from the court.

The court proceedings lasted two full years, and seven more months passed before the judgment was given. It is true that the extraordinary length of the trial was partly due to the extensiveness of the subjects at issue. But the peculiar multi-language system of the court had much more to do with the delay. The court proceeded both in English and Japanese, while any one speaking in the court was required to use his own native language—German, French, Dutch, Spanish, Chinese, Annanese, etc., etc.—which was at once translated into English and Japanese. But the incommensurability of the English and the Japanese language, in both speech psychology and grammatical construction, was such that, in the court room, any of the interpreters always had to wait for the speaker to come to a full stop, then take apart all the elements of thought and speech and re-arrange them according to the rules of thought and speech of the other language. Even for skilled interpreters it took time to do that.

In the translators' room behind the scene, the same difficulty existed. In the busiest period of the defense, there were more than fifty people of various ages and past careers working in our office. Ex-college teachers who had found their teaching salaries too small, ex-diplomats, ex-language officers in the Japanese Army and Navy, ex-employees of foreign trade companies and shipping firms, all of whom had lost jobs with the fall of the Japanese Empire, worked side by side with young boys and girls just out of or still in college. At first all the translators, irrespective of age and past career, were treated on the same footing, and the Allied officers directly supervised the work of each of us, but they soon found it impracticable. So the translators came to be grouped into several teams with a top worker assigned to each group to help check the translations of its members. In this way I came to supervise the work of several young people. The practical result was that I had to rewrite many of the manuscripts handed over to me for checking, and had in consequence to carry on several people's work. The fault lay not so much in the unskilled translators, as in the fundamental differences between the Japanese and the English language.

This peculiar language of the Japanese people, apparently completely unrelated to any of the language groups of the human races, is causing grave difficulties to its speakers and writers, particularly in these days of international closeness. It is not only insular but totally under-developed from the present world's point of view. Japanese people themselves are struggling hard to hammer this quaintly formed language into a workable modern tool of self-expression. They often despair. To express a series of modern ideas in Japanese is difficult enough. To translate such ideas from Japanese into English is not simply a matter of linguistic skill. It requires a revolution in the human mind.

In the Japanese language exactness of expression is purposely avoided. Suggestiveness is valued in our speech, as it is indispensable in our art. Even in talking of an exact time or number, it is quite common to say, "I spotted the plane *around* 25 minutes 47 seconds past 2 p.m." and "You owe me *about* 7 dollars and 59 cents." From this vagueness comes a further peculiarity. We drop off the subject and the object wherever the presence or absence of honorifics and other modulatory expressions of respect, non-respect or contempt is sufficient to show who or what is being talked about. But this elliptical method is too often abused, and in the handling of a complex group of ideas it causes utter confusion. At best it only serves to strengthen the subjectivity of the writing, so that a Japanese reader has always to put himself in the position and frame of mind of the writer himself before he can follow the writer's words.

The greatest difficulty modern Japanese prose writing faces is the weakness in the syntax of modifiers. There being no relative conjunctives, a profuse amount of phrases and clauses are usually hung together on loose, slippery connectives. The reader is left to himself to puzzle out their respective positions in thought sequence. The Japanese language harmonizes with the expression of lyrical or linear thought, and may go so far as to serve for the two-dimensional presentation of ideas. But beyond that, for multi-dimensional, synthetical composition, it totally fails and results in a jumble of mutilated phrases. In modern Japanese prose writing of ordinary levels, the reader feels as if he were being led blindfolded through a maze with only a stick to guide his steps.

These peculiar traits of our language require an agile brain and a mature mind to read and understand the content of Japanese writing clearly enough so that the same content of ideas may be translated into English. Skill in Japanese-English translation is therefore a matter not of methodical training, but of an ability to think and express the same thoughts and ideas on two fundamentally different planes of language psychology and construction. An efficient Japanese-English translator needs a magician's skill.

There are also some grave technical difficulties. First of all, the Japanese language has no singular and plural forms which in any way correspond to the singular and plural nouns in the English language. A Japanese singular generally means distinction, and a plural indistinction. A modest person alludes to himself as "we" instead of "I" and a conceited husband may call to his wife, "Hey, you wives!" It is absolutely impossible to write English without being sure whether a given noun is singular or plural. Consequently, even when all other points are clear in the meaning of the Japanese text, the singular-or-plural question constantly holds up the translator. In connection with nouns, the English articles puzzle and exasperate a Japanese mind. The articles offer us a source of infinite fascination because they are totally absent in our language. But the grammatical singular and plural in English nouns seem terribly mechanical to us. We protestingly ask why "one apple" should be so distinguished and "two apples" and "a million apples" should wear the same grammatical liveries.

Another exasperating peculiarity of the Japanese language is that in its written form, it uses Chinese characters mixed with Japanese letters in the most arbitrary, unsystematic manner. Each character is pronounced sometimes more than a dozen widely differing ways. In cases of proper names, this usage becomes outrageous. You may know how a personal or place name is written out, but may not know exactly how it is read, and so are totally at a loss how to transcribe it in Roman letters. How could a trial proceed when the names of persons and places involved were Romanized in half a dozen different ways?

It did frequently happen in court that English translations or interpretations of identical Japanese passages in the Prosecution and the Defense Section differed widely or were even completely opposed in meaning. The Language Arbitration Board, after painstaking reviewing, had to decide which was correct.

Despite the great size of our office staff, our translation work did not progress speedily. Once or twice the Court had to be temporarily adjourned because we couldn't keep pace with the court proceedings. At any rate, we all grappled hard with huge amounts of evidence, testimonial depositions and reference material, most of which were in Japanese writing of the most involved style, which taxed our English writing ability to the utmost.

But I was sincerely happy to work there and so apparently was every Japanese worker I came to know in the Defense Section. We were all surprised to find that the American lawyers who had volunteered cooperation and guidance for the Japanese defense counsel there, were far more sympathetic than the Japanese people themselves for the tragic situation of the defendants. The Allied officers in charge of the work and management of the Section were also friendly, often to the point of indulgence, toward the Japanese employees. There were just a few "off limits" regulations maintained there, but these were merely matters of form and never of sentiment.

When, after two full years of session, the court adjourned for the last time on April 16, 1948, only to meet again on the day of judgment, excitement held us tight. Some translators in the Defense Section were transferred to the direct employment of the Tribunal for the Japanese translation of the verdicts and sentences to be given out in English. The translation staff, together with typists, stenographers, mimeographing helpers, cooks and maids, was confined in a single house appropriated for the purpose. It lived in complete separation from the rest of the world within barbed wire fences guarded by American military police. I did not join the group, but many women, including a number of married women, most willingly did, because the pay was good and included all the meals throughout the term of confinement.

Assurance of good meals meant a great deal to Japanese people at that time.

The confinement was at first expected to last some six weeks. But apparently the judges of the tribunal talked and deliberated on and on, while the translation staff awaited immediate action. The entire Japanese people held its breath over the imminent fates of their former national leaders.

At last, on November 12, 1948, four months after the confinement of the translators was started and seven months after the adjournment of the court, the judgment was pronounced. Five army generals and one diplomat-statesman were sentenced to death, seventeen got life imprisonment, and two limited punishment. The people in general had expected more death sentences, so apparently they felt relieved at the actual number, although sorry for the six condemned prisoners—particularly the single non-military statesman. Defense counsel once more got busy and petitioned the Supreme Commander to review and reconsider the sentences. But evidently no change whatsoever was effected in any of the sentences. One snowy midnight in early 1949, the executions were carried out.

The people in general, occupied with more urgent questions of daily life, had not much time to dwell on the results of these Major War Crimes Trials, and shortly put them out of their minds altogether. However, some Japanese felt extremely disappointed when our newspapers published the last words of the executed prisoners, which had to do with the transience of human life (in the traditional tone of the dying heroes of our feudal history) instead of expressing regret at having failed the

Japanese people and caused such harm to humanity. Perhaps some of them were regretful, but the newspapers did not report the fact, intentionally or unintentionally. I remember that General Yamashita was reported in the papers, or at least in a leading paper, as begging the pardon of his people, just before he was executed at Manila. I wish our major war criminals had expressed in some way their apology, at least toward the Japanese people. It would have demonstrated to the people the basic principles of democracy, and would have been a slight recompense for the two billion yen the bankrupt nation according to the newspaper report of the time, had spent as their share in the trials.

As it happened, the major leaders of our tragic war have already faded away completely into the past, into the category of our feudal heroes. They have left nothing, unless it is bitterness, in the minds of the people who are now struggling hard to recover from the losses of the war, and to stand on a solid democratic footing.

12. Consequences

After the dissolution of the International Military Tribunal for the Far East, I found employment, again as a translator, in the Defense Section of the War Crimes Tribunal. This had been newly organized for the trials of the former chiefs of the Naval Staff, and of the Prisoners of War Management Department of the War Ministry. Both were held responsible for the atrocities committed by the Japanese Army and Navy during the war.

The two accused were tried separately. I worked mainly for Admiral Toyoda's American Defense Counsel. The defense staff consisted of two American and three Japanese lawyers, several translators, interpreters, typists, and a head business manager. Nearly all of these had moved over from the Major War Crimes Trials and they worked in perfect harmony and cooperation. The two American lawyers, both Harvard men, were hard-working, energetic, high minded advocates of international justice and fairness. The Japanese staff, completely captivated by them, most willingly and happily followed their lead. While working for them, I learned something about the method and spirit of the law courts of a democratic country, which proved very useful to me later.

The trial lasted nearly eleven months, although this time the proceedings were carried on in English alone, Japanese being used only when necessary. The prosecution and the defense fought most spiritedly. The defense counsel spared no pains whatsoever to supply even the smallest of their points with ample evidence and witnesses, and was always ready for thorough rebuttal. The basic claim of the defense was that the Japanese Navy was so organized that the posts of the Commander-in-chief of the Combined Fleet, and of the Chief of the Naval Staff, the two last and most important positions the defendants held while serving in the Japanese Navy, had to do exclusively with the tactical command of the operational forces, while the management of prisoners of war and the government of the people of the occupied territories were matters of pure military administration. The Tribunal accepted this claim of the defense as valid, and acquitted the defendant of all charges, to the joy of the entire nation.

While I was working for the International Military Tribunal for the Far East, and for Admiral Toyoda's trial, I was often asked to translate into English various petitions to be submitted to the Allied authorities. These were mostly in connection with the war crimes trials, and in this way I came to handle petitions relating to two death sentence cases.

One was the case of a lieutenant general tried and sentenced by the Netherland military court in Hollandia, New Guinea. His wife and friends petitioned for the commutation of his sentence. From the first interview I liked his wife very much. He was comparatively advanced in age, and he had been a mere division-commander, stationed at a remote outpost which was cut off from all supply lines. I felt therefore that I could tell that whatever criminal acts he had been judged guilty of had been committed under unavoidable circumstances as far as he was concerned. Most willingly I translated many long petitions for him. I was terribly upset when his wife told me he had become ill and died in prison.

The other instance concerned a doctor involved in the awful vivisection case. He was an assistant-professor, and the favorite pupil of the head professor of the surgical division in the medical department of Kyushu Imperial University, where these criminal operations were conducted under the command of the military. He had joined the medical faculty of the university at the invitation of the head of the surgical division several months before the unhappy event occurred. The special favor shown to him by the division head had incurred the envy and hostility of some of his colleagues.

One day soon after his return home from a visit to his sick mother in his native village, he was ordered to attend a surgical operation on a prisoner of war. When he saw what was going on, he was horrified. He was a good Buddhist. When he was ordered to attend a second time, he objected to the act from his Buddhist-humanist point of view. The head professor would not listen to his remonstrations and insisted he attend. In Japan, at that time, disobedience to authority in a government university was on a par with disobedience in the Army. So he went quite late, hoping that everything would be over, but the second operation lasted longer than the first, and he arrived in the midst of it. He definitely refused, however, to attend the last two operations and finally the head professor exempted him from the duty.

When the matter was brought to the notice of the Occupation authorities after the close of the war, the head professor committed suicide just before he was to be arrested. The doctors and military officers who took leading roles in the event did their best to cover up evidence. But Dr. Torisu, the Buddhist doctor, was not apprehensive, and even agreed to allow the defense counsel to withhold the fact from the court that he had deliberately refused to attend the last two operations. He was told that this fact would put some of the co-defendants who had wilfully participated in all of the criminal acts in a very unfavorable light. So when he was questioned on the witness-stand by the prosecution counsel whether it was through his own choice that he did not attend the last two operations, he simply said that business had called him elsewhere on both of these occasions.

Mrs. Torisu, whose husband had told her what he had seen and done in connection with the first two operations immediately after each event, and who knew that he had intentionally avoided the subsequent undertakings, was promised by the defense counsel a chance to testify in court. Later this was refused. Evidently the defense counsel had changed its policy and decided to sacrifice Dr. Torisu for the benefit of some other defendants.

The joint trial of more than 30 accused—army officers, doctors, medical students, nurses and clerks—went on for five months, I think. The horrors of the criminal acts were brought to public notice. However, as I was told later by an officer of the Legal Section of GHQ, of all the war crime cases tried under the Occupation, the truth in this matter was concealed most tenaciously to the very end. Evidently the defense counsel stuck to the least-said-the-quickest-mended policy, and did not use even a single witness outside the defendants themselves. The result was that the Military Court of Yokohama sentenced to death three doctors—Dr. Torisu and the two doctors whom the defense counsel was particularly anxious to save—and some army officers.

When Mrs. Torisu came up to Tokyo to petition for the commutation of her husband's sentence, she got to know a friend of mine, who asked me to help her. This was in the spring of

1948, when I was working for Admiral Toyoda's trial. I translated her petitions into English and accompanied her, as interpreter, to see the officers of the Legal Section and the Reviewing Board of GHQ. She could not stay long in Tokyo because her home was in Fukuoka, in the western end of Japan, where she taught school in order to support her three children and herself in the face of postwar inflation. She came up to Tokyo whenever she could, and apparently her husband's friends financed her frequent and expensive trips.

In order to explain the complicated circumstances which had led to the court's misjudgment of her husband's case, Mrs. Torisu had to write many petitions and make clear every point of doubt held by the Reviewing Board. At first her petitions had the tone of appealing to the "mercy" of the Supreme Commander of the Allied Powers. My previous experience with the defense cases of the war crimes trials had taught me that "justice based on truth" is all-important in the law courts of a democratic country. After talking with Mrs. Torisu once, and corresponding with her husband in Sugamo Prison, I was convinced that they were both honest people who, during the trial, had neither felt the necessity nor had money for behind-the-scene activities. So I advised her to state the whole truth and demand of the Supreme Commander justice, not mercy. In an absolute monarchy, the ruler's mercy and justice are practically identical. But in a democracy, mercy is sought only by self-admitted sinners and criminals.

I also discovered that Mrs. Torisu was afraid to tell the whole truth about the unfair treatment her husband had received from the defense counsel because this defense counsel included some American members. She feared that the officers of the reviewing board would not be pleased to hear anything said against their countrymen. But I was confident that in American minds the idea of justice was impersonal and above such personal sentiment as nationalism. I encouraged her to tell everything, because it was the only way to save her husband's life.

The Occupation law officers listened to Mrs. Torisu's explanations and read her petitions most attentively. Yet she lived in constant fear that her efforts would be in vain and that the report of her husband's execution would be brought to her any day. There had been such instances before, she said. She got more and more nervous and restless and was harassed by horrible dreams.

Evidently the case was of such an unusual and terrible nature that it required the longest and most careful re-examination of all the cases brought before the Reviewing Board. After a year and a half of our hard work and anxious and painful waiting, and more than two years after the pronouncement of the judgment, Dr. Torisu's death-sentence was commuted to a ten-year imprisonment. This was one of the happiest moments of my life. I was thanked not only by Dr. Torisu and his family and friends, but also by some GHQ law officers for my cooperation.

If I did help the Occupation authorities with regard to the just commutation of Dr. Torisu's death-sentence, it was through my ability—inadequate as it was—to think on two different planes of language psychology and express Japanese ideas in Anglo-

American terms of justice. This language barrier between those who judged and those who were judged must have caused numerous instances of misunderstanding and misjudgment, particularly in cases where it was hard to trace to particular individuals the responsibility for criminal acts committed by the Japanese forces overseas and at home on the eve of the collapse of our entire military system.

A collection of letters and notes of dead student-soldiers of the last war, recently published, includes letters written home by a young man who was executed as a war criminal on one of the South Pacific bases. This young man had to promise his superior that he would not testify against him. He kept his word at the trial. It is not clear from the letters exactly what he had done, but he was sentenced to death. In one of the letters he denounces the cowardice of his superior in pretending complete ignorance of the subordinate's terrible sacrifice. So he wrote a petition in English which explained his situation, but somehow —very probably because of his inadequate English—no attention was paid to it.

The young man now prepares himself for the execution. He pores over the book of philosophy he has with him—a book written by a contemporary philosopher and widely read by students of the time—and finds therein solutions for the problems of life, death and the eternity he is now facing. He never complains of his misfortune. He tells his family not to grieve. "After all," he writes, "what is demanded by the war crimes court is the lives of Japanese soldiers in equal number to the prisoners our unit killed. They are not, nor can they be, very particular about which of us it shall be." He accepts his lot calmly and even with sincere contentment. His dignity and modesty of behavior in the prison impresses the guards. Consequently, they treat him with respect and gentleness, although they act toward many other prisoners with a spirit of retaliation for what Japanese guards had once done toward the Allied prisoners.

"We are all human beings," he writes, "who can, irrespective of racial and language differences, see what is truly good in each other." And he prays for the coming of the time when human beings may not be forced to kill each other—at least when they do not hate each other.

When the day of his execution approaches, he writes again to his family. He came from a happy, well-to-do family. He asks them to build him a grave on a sunny hillside and to offer to his spirit on every anniversary of his death gay flowers and his favorite French pastry, and to remember that he died in perfect contentment of soul. He then thanks the heaven and the earth and his family for the good life they have given him in this world. He resents nothing except the corruption of the Japanese Army. In his last 31-syllable poem he writes that, "I am returning today to the sweet breast of my beloved Mother," and he meets Eternity on the scaffold.

From the western humanistic and democratic point of view, this young man's conduct may be criticized as deserving death because he did not object to the inhuman act when he was ordered to commit it. Moreover, he should have told the whole truth to the court, instead of withholding the fact of his superior's responsibility. But in the Japanese army, disobedience was absolutely impossible. To protect another's fault, whether or not at one's own cost, was and still is considered a noble act in the semi-feudal ethical system of the Japanese people, where justice is still too often personal and arbitrary, and where the assertion of individual rights and responsibilities is not clearly distinguished from an act of selfishness.

This may appear most distasteful to the Western sense of justice. But among the Japanese people falsehood is leniently looked on if it is used for the kindly purpose of concealing another's guilt. Leniency of this kind, however, is apt to instigate perjury for the sake of one's own defense. Moreover, the Japanese people's "Yes" and "No" are still largely motivated by their traditional self-effacing habit of saying things, not from a sense of individual responsibility or truthfulness, but largely from their feeling toward the environment.

Recently a case was reported which illustrated this collective sentiment of the Japanese people. In a diet election, a dishonest method was used in a certain village, and a young girl of the same village, witnessing it, truthfully reported it to the judiciary authorities of the prefecture, which thereupon fined the offenders. The entire village, however, boycotted the girl and her family socially and economically, declaring that although they admitted the dishonesty of the conduct of some of them in the election, the girl had no business to disclose this dishonesty to the outside world. The issue has been taken up by some progressive minded people. But the democratic battle started by them has—even in this seventh year after the fall of our feudal militarism—hardly even made a scratch on the hard-shelled collectivism of rural Japan.

These peculiarly non-individualistic traits of our people apparently worked to an exasperating extent at every one of the War Crimes Courts. Petition upon petition came in after the trials were over. One of the GHQ law officers said to me once, "I wish they had spoken out about these things when they were given the chance in court, instead of howling and twittering in these thousands of petitions!" I can understand and sympathize with both sides. And although I feel sure that many were rightly punished, I cannot but fear that as a fatal result of this peculiar mentality as well as the language difficulty of the Japanese people, not only the student-soldier and Dr. Torisu, but a number of other good men, were sentenced to undeserved punishment.

Another boy comes to mind in connection with the war crimes trials. He was the Nisei Canadian-Japanese husband of the lovely Chinese girl I met on the street in the midst of the air-raid on Tokyo. After the close of the war the girl got a good position in one of the offices of the Occupation Army because of her Allied nationality and perfect command of English. She once invited me to her new apartment and treated me to a superb dinner and some gifts. Finding her well off now, I stopped going to see her as often as I had used to.

But I asked about her husband whenever I came across any one returning from the South Pacific. "An interpreter in a military police headquarters?" a man asked me gravely. Army interpreters were the very first to be prosecuted by the war crimes courts, he explained, because during the way they attended to the actual business of the management of Allied prisoners, and only those who had protected the prisoners at the risk of their own lives and who had subsequently been given letters of thanks by such prisoners, were acquitted. He himself was such an ex-army interpreter. He had not been able, however, to be good to all the prisoners unconditionally, so he was still in constant fear of being called back to the trial. An interpreter in a military police office was in the worst situation, he added.

I later met another young ex-army interpreter returning from a South Pacific island in the same circumstances as the first young man. He told me that I could easily find out at the Demobilization Office about the Nisei boy I was asking about, but I did not feel anxious to go there.

Quite unexpectedly, after a long interval, I met the Chinese girl on the street last summer. "I met a friend of my husband's sometime ago," she said. I had purposely avoided alluding to her husband, but since she took the initiative, I anxiously asked what had become of him. "O, they hanged him," she said with a hard, forlorn face.

I remember her telling me that her husband, who had been called to service while studying in a college in Tokyo, disliked his work with the Military Police and finally obtained a discharge on the excuse of his poor health. She also told me that he was so homesick for his native land of Canada that he was planning to go back there with her when the war was over. The single miscarriage in his plan that prevented him from taking the same boat with his wife to the homeland of Japan led to his destruction.

I have often been asked by my American friends if I saw anything worth while in the setting up of "those shows," meaning the war crimes trials. Every time I have answered "Yes." First of all, they disclosed to the otherwise ignorant Japanese people all the defects of our nationalistic militarism. The voluminous verdicts of the Major War Crimes Tribunal especially have given us an authentic, judicious, detailed history of Japanese imperialism from the Manchurian Affair to its downfall, which no contemporary Japanese historian could have ever written.

As for the vindication of international justice, for which the war crimes trials were primarily intended, we may say that some elementary steps have been achieved. The Japanese people in general were impressed by the sincere attempts at justice which were made by the Major War Crimes Tribunal, as well as by the courtesy it showed to the defendants and their families. They were, as a whole, satisfied with, or at least found the results of the trials comprehensible. It seems, however, that in some of the military courts of the South Pacific bases, where there was neither time nor means to be as judicious and as circumspect as the Major Tribunal at Tokyo, justice was administered solely

and concisely on the Western democratic premises, so foreign
to the average Japanese mind. Prisoners, as well as the Japanese
people in general, got the impression that in those courts international justice quite often stood on an elementary eye-for-an-
eye level.

Part Four

POSTWAR FAMILY QUESTIONS

13. Shattering Family Traditions

The war brought to Japan both economic bankruptcy and the bankruptcy of our social traditions. In the economic and social anarchy that followed, every one, except just a few strangely tucked-away individuals, had to pick up a living by himself. An old man of eighty and a child of ten had the same problem. Any one who failed simply dropped out of life. This desperate situation helped to foster a basic democratic tendency, and worked as the principal factor for the shattering of our feudalistic family system. It resulted in the independence and unmanageableness of the younger generation. This, of all the radical postwar changes, has most immediately affected our family life.

Very few parents of the former upper and middle classes were still able to send their children to college or even high school without the children themselves earning at least a part of their expenses. Japanese boys, once brought up never to talk about money and trade, now blackmarketed among themselves, sold newspapers and peddled peanuts in the street. Women and girls of all ages knitted and sewed for money, embroidered gloves, table-cloths and handkerchiefs, and made artificial flowers for export brokers at frightfully cheap wages. Their homes were in many cases a tiny room or two where six, seven or more people lived together, stepping upon each other and sleeping in "fishes-in-a-basket" fashion. The parents under these circumstances could not very well be too dignified before the children, nor could they reasonably tell them to stay home instead of going out into the confusion and immorality of the street. The Japanese people had lost all class distinctions and sunk into practically uniform poverty and sordidness.

We were lucky to have found a house to live in by ourselves, and my husband and I had incomes large enough to keep our children alive. The gift packages from America enabled me to clothe them handsomely. But beyond that, the children had to take care of themselves. For a while at least, we could not possibly keep careful watch on what they did to get a note-book, a pair of canvas shoes, or even books they needed at school.

The older of the two boys was several months below the deadline when all college students above a certain age, excepting special science students, were enlisted and sent over to the battlefronts. So he finished college, though in a very haphazard way, in the midst of the wartime and postwar confusions.

My eldest daughter was graduated from Tokyo Women's

Medical College just as the war ended, and at once began her internship as a nose and ear specialist in a hospital. The next year she got married.

During her first year at the medical college she began to attend a Protestant Christian church in our neighborhood. Shortly afterward she was baptized there. The minister's wife was a charming American woman, who worked most courageously and patiently for the church all through the war. Our families were on friendly and sympathetic terms, and all my family were baptized in her church at one time or another during the war. There my daughter met a boy, who soon after finishing college, was called to military service as a language officer and some time later went to Manchuria. Then we heard nothing more of him, even after the close of the war. We were not sure whether he was alive.

One day in the third summer of the Occupation, he suddenly appeared at our door. He was just back from Dairen where he had been kept prisoner since the close of the war. Kazuko was at the hospital. Our younger daughter rushed out of the house, ran all the way to the electric railway station and from the last station to the hospital and brought her sister home. There was no telephone working in our neighborhood then.

That evening Kazuko went out with him and when they came back, they announced their engagement. We accepted the event as a matter of course, as we had known that they had been interested in each other and we had liked the boy. We were all excited, because this was the first engagement in our family.

Personally I had not known this boy well enough to be wholeheartedly happy or anything else about this engagement. Grandmother had known him much better than I, because Kazuko had lived most of the time with her before the air-raids. Probably the old lady was the most pleased person in the family about the turn of events.

What occupied my mind more urgently was how to get the two young people married and set up in a new household in the midst of the hard conditions we were then facing. Kazuko was taking another year of internship in pediatrics. In a year or so she would be earning money as a qualified doctor. The boy, whose parents were dead had no place to go. He got a job in one of the foreign trading companies which were shooting up in the postwar trade boom, and felt he was ready to marry if only he could find a house, or at least a room. Finding a house or even a single room to live in was out of the question in the Tokyo of these times. Most parts were still waste lands where people lived in whatever shelters they could find. Since there was no knowing how long we would have to wait before we could regain a normal way of life, we finally decided that they should be married as soon as possible, and live with us in our house.

The next problem was how to celebrate the wedding. To buy a ceremonial kimono for the bride was out of the question. Not a yard of silk, cotton or any other kind of fabric was obtainable except at fabulous blackmarket prices. Kazuko decided to borrow from a married friend of hers a Western-style white dress and all the necessary accessories. I gave her the dresses, shoes, blankets, towels and soap I had been given by my American friends. Without these kind gifts my girl could not have obtained a single thing—even a piece of soap or a spool of sewing thread—for her marriage trousseau. I was sincerely grateful for them.

The bridegroom was to wear his father's frock coat which, together with some other things, his uncle had kept safely for him. Grandmother was very anxious that all the family, at least the grown-ups, should wear proper ceremonial clothes. But none of us, including even the old lady, had been careful enough to save our ceremonial robes from the fire. So we all borrowed from our friends.

Toward the end of 1947, the wedding ceremony was performed at the Christian church to which the young couple belonged. A reception and tea were given at our house. Many of our women guests wore baggy mompé trousers over their beautiful ceremonial kimono and brocade obi for traveling across the city in tight-packed cars. They presented peculiar figures, but it was the only way for them to protect their precious clothes from the ruinous traffic rush.

Our tea was a great success. At first we were dismayed at the thought of how to get refreshments for the party. Food was still treated as a thing to keep one barely alive. Anything above the minimum subsistence level involved blackmarket procedure and a fabulous amount of money. Most unexpectedly then a package arrived from America, containing everything we could wish for—beautiful flour, sugar, powdered milk and egg, bars of chocolate and a box of lovely, colorful candies! The minister's American wife was as delighted as I was. With these supplies, and plenty of her own, she baked three beautiful wedding cakes.

She also let us use the plates and teacups belonging to the church. At the last moment an American friend in Tokyo gave me another big box of luscious chocolate candy.

Some fifteen guests and six members of the family sat around the married pair in our two tiny upstairs rooms, cleared for the occasion of the rickety furniture and unseemly piles of books we had collected since the close of the war. The American cakes and candies surprised and delighted every one. The saccharined black tea we served was the only thing we had to buy from the expensive black market for that grand tea party.

The next day the married couple went on a short honeymoon trip to a hot springs. They carried a bag of rice with them and stayed overnight in a boarding house belonging to a certain labor union. Our girl was twenty-five then.

So our first family wedding was carried out in a very satisfactory manner as far as the strained circumstances of the time were considered. But the grandmother, who was really satisfied with what had been done for the occasion, on the other hand must have sadly reflected on this "patched up" wedding party of her granddaughter's as compared to the pomp and ceremony and grand display in which her son's nuptials were celebrated, and the luxury and aristocratic atmosphere in which that granddaughter was born as the idol of the family. As for me, not so well acquainted with the past glory of the family, and very realistic for the present, I simply felt grateful that Kazuko had chosen her husband by herself and thereby relieved me of the awful labor and responsibility of hunting up a good man for her. I was also grateful for my American connections, which had enabled me to take care of the wedding celebration.

I was also realistic enough to take it as a matter of course when Kazuko called her husband by his plain name instead of calling him "my lord" or "master." She insisted on acting on equal terms with him. Her grandmother was shocked at first but soon accepted this postwar form of family status. And the young man seemed to be willing to do so, too.

Shortly after her marriage, Kazuko got a paying position in another hospital. At the end of that year a baby girl arrived. With a baby to care for, she found it impossible to continue her work in the hospital. After various experiments at adjustment, she finally decided, with the encouragement of her husband, to open a clinic office at home. Our house was already crowded enough, but there being no alternative, we spared another of our rooms for her use. She and her husband borrowed money to obtain the necessary equipment.

When her baby was hardly a year old, she found her husband developing a tendency to tuberculosis. We had known that he had not been very strong since his childhood, but since he had withstood with apparent health two years of strenuous military life and another two years of imprisonment in Manchuria, we had thought him strong enough to marry. Our house was too crowded for him, and every sanitorium we went to had a waiting list so long that a new applicant might have to wait a full year. Even in our neighborhood alone we knew some half a dozen tuberculosis patients, unable to be hospitalized, who lay in crowded homes, and shared the same room with other people. The outlook was dismal.

Just then our minister's American wife introduced us to the LARA organization (licensed agencies for Relief in Asia). Through this organization she got us a full amount of streptomycin free of charge at a time when that medicine cost more than a thousand yen a gram in Japan. Shortly after, through the kindness of a friend of mine, our son-in-law was accepted in a sanitorium run by the Salvation Army at a beautiful location outside Tokyo. He stayed there for a year and a half and thoroughly recovered. All the while the national health insurance system, newly introduced under the Occupation, kept us free from financial worries.

The young man has recently come home, having recovered enough to live in the crowded house again, and to resume the work of a person of normal health. He is happy and grateful, but the difficulty is that a man with a sanitorium record is treated with caution at any employment office, and is brushed aside for young men in perfect health who are just out of well-reputed universities and have good records and favorable family connections. In the sharp competition of the Japanese business world, this group alone gets jobs considered worth while—at least from the Japanese standard.

It is true that our government now is taking better care of our tuberculosis patients. Conditions have markedly improved since the days of postwar confusion. But their employment problem remains as bad as ever. Our son-in-law told us of one man who, after spending ten years in a sanitorium, came back to the world, but could find no means of supporting himself and so committed suicide.

Meanwhile, our daughter has grown into an efficient doctor, very popular in the neighborhood because of her kindness, thoroughness, and because her charges are strictly on health insurance standards. She now earns enough to support herself, her husband and daughter decently enough, despite the seven different taxes she has to pay—including one on her microscope, stethoscope, scissors, pincets and other tools of her trade. Her success as a doctor owes much to her grandmother's selfless devotion. The old lady cooks and takes care of her baby as well as her husband, while she sees her patients or goes out to attend medical lectures and doctors' meetings. She cannot hire domestic help because food costs so much, and because our house is so packed that it cannot hold another person. So her grandmother keeps busy all the time, and though over seventy now, she says she will live another ten years and work as much as she can for her dear granddaughter and her little girl and possibly some more children of hers.

Sometimes I get jealous of my stepdaughter because she has such whole-hearted assistance from her grandmother, who refused to help me when I had to teach and tutor English ten hours a day, and had to give up having children of my own, as well as my reading and writing hobby, in order to help my husband support the family. But I am happy to have recommended a medical career to her, and grateful for her having followed my advice. Medicine just suits her, and gives her strength and charm.

Kazuko is a woman always motivated by a sense of duty and selflessness. Her personal likes and dislikes are completely subdued and almost never motivate her action. She is nearly always at peace with everybody. However, she is afraid to make up her own mind and waits for some one to tell her what to do. On the other hand, she has a high moral standard, and she finds the Christian teachings a congenial guiding force, and her profession full of great human duties. Guided by the Bible and equipped with medical training, this small, delicate, sweet-looking woman will continue to grow in goodness, helpfulness and strength.

14. Liberalism at Home

Our two boys presented more serious problems than their good Christian sister. During the war both of them followed their sister's lead and diligently attended church with her. The older boy became deeply interested in Protestant Christianity and one summer he attended the camp meetings of Dr. Yanaibara, a prominent Christian leader who is now president of Tokyo University. He also made a pilgrimage to Kyoto and Nara to see with his own eyes the legacies of beauty of our ancient Buddhist culture. Food conditions were so bad at that time that during his travels he was lucky indeed if he got a meal a day. He did not know how much time was left to him before he would be called to war, so he was trying to make a quick gauge of humanity and of Japanese culture.

He went through the conscripts' examinations and was enlisted for an air-base maintenance corps, but before he was called, the war ended. He returned home from the naval supply depot where he had been working with the rest of his university classmates. The turn of events was too overwhelming. He gave up Christianity, philosophy and art, and turned to the labor movement. He did not attend the classes now reopened at Tokyo University, partly because he had lost interest in "old things" and partly because he now had to work both for his living and university expenses. It took him two more years to complete the university course. Then he got a job in a publishing house.

The younger boy had already been a cause of greater anxiety for us. After finishing high school, he wandered around trying to be a singer, stage actor, movie actor, producer and so on. He got into the habit of excessive smoking and coffee-drinking, which took a frightful amount of money since both tobacco and coffee were tightly controlled luxuries. We urged him to try a college entrance examination. He passed, but he did not seem to be very anxious to study, and we did not feel rich enough to push and prod him along this expensive path. He soon dropped out.

Then came the lure of communism. The clear cut theory and ideology of Marxian socialism were evidently very attractive to the war-devastated minds of Japanese youth. My two boys were no exception. They began to follow the leftist groups in our neighborhood. Soon I found that nearly all of my older boy's best university friends were showing similar tendencies. My husband and I warned the boys, but we had an idea then that democracy was far stronger than communism, and that it would swallow up communist ideas and digest them into its flesh and blood. Communism had just been made legal in Japan by the newly promulgated democratic constitution of the nation. So we decided that the boys were free to act according to their conscience and on their own responsibility. I often argued quite heatedly with my older boy about communistic materialism and my idea of "the realm of the human soul." Neither of us yielded, but we both agreed to respect each other's freedom of thought.

In the early days of the Occupation there was no clear distinction in the minds of most Japanese people between communism and democracy. Both of them were ideals and practices of the Allied countries and had been simultaneously propagated in this country, just liberated from the curse of a desperate fascism. Only, communism was easier for them to understand and follow. Despite the enthusiastic and drastic democratization measures of the Occupation government, and despite the fact that almost every Japanese was daily talking about "democracy," very few of them understood what this wonderful word really meant. It was a remarkable experience, indeed, for a Japanese to find himself in a line of young men and women in happy pairs, workmen in soiled khaki, old women with walking canes, and mothers with babies on their backs, streaming to the ballot box, to vote in the first postwar national election. Any one could see that it was democracy at work. But aside from occasional democratic events of such constitutional nature, our life continued to be full of the old difficulties. Our national government did not tell us exactly how or in what democratic way our troubled national life was going to be bettered.

The communists, on the other hand, got down directly to the problems of daily life. They talked loudly about our food and housing problems, traffic jams, and unfair taxes, and pointed out concrete methods of removing these troubles. Whether these ways were practicable or not, they served as useful propaganda. To sway educated people, moreover, they preached the historical necessity of the downfall of Japanese feudalistic-capitalistic imperialism, and the inevitability of the people's government. Not a few thoughtful Japanese felt somewhat convinced of the reasonableness of their views.

Communism, in this way, came to be ardently followed by young idealistic people and by elderly men of youthful zest. Lovers of power and leadership eagerly embraced it, and the discontented masses viewed it sympathetically. The Japan Communist Party swelled its ranks quickly by taking in all kinds of individuals, and gathering sympathizers of various tastes and inclinations around it.

The ideal and aim of the Japanese communists at that time were evidently to win the trust and affection of the people. If they once got the love and support of the people, they thought, they could gain political power through constitutional steps rather than by disagreeable illegal methods. So they decided that they must look and act pleasantly so that dread of the Communist Party, inculcated in the minds of the people by the crafty, capitalist-militarist-police government of the former days, would disappear.

Good clothes and the enjoyment of life were no longer enemies of the proletariat. Look at the Russians. With the growth of their wonderful socialistic economy their living standards had been remarkably raised and they now had the good things of life. Japanese communists were generally attentive to dress and were determined not to fall behind the rest of the people in sociable enjoyment of the return of peace and the downfall of Japanese imperialism. So they gave dancing parties wherever they could find a room large enough, which was not easy since almost all of the sizable houses, public or private, which had escaped bombing, had been handed over for Occupation use, or were packed to the brim with Japanese occupants. The postwar dancing mania was nation-wide and Communists catching it not only demonstrated to the general public that Communists were just as human as the rest of humanity, but also contributed a great deal toward their fund campaigns, for tickets for social dancing under whatever auspices sold very well at that time.

Even the Japanese "bourgeois" papers once ran a picture of a communist dance where the bald-headed "Number One" leader was shown proudly leading a handsome, extremely well-dressed girl recently back from Moscow. And to the observation of the insular Japanese eye, there was no essential difference in the women's dress styles in Moscow, Paris or New York.

There was nothing strange about all this, some Orientalists commented, because Western Democracy and Russian Communism were only two somewhat varying products of the same machine civilization of the Western World. The Oriental countries had an essentially different system of civilization.

At any rate, the Japanese Communists of the time had plenty of easygoing hopes and merry laughter in their hearts. Middle-class vanities and humor played a part in their social life despite the hard language they hurled on the petty bourgeoisie.

An anxious mother once confided to me that she was sincerely grateful for the Communist influence keeping her touchy, sensitive boy busy within its bounds, for it was the only place which, with its high social and moral preachings, kept young boys from stealing, swindling, gambling, brawling, black-marketeering, black-mailing and all other terrible postwar immoralities. I quite agreed with her for the sake of my boys, particularly the younger one. She went on to say that her boy was well guarded from girls, because he would not easily fall in love with any of the leftist girls he associated with, nor would those political-minded young women readily get romantic. I then remembered my younger boy's comment, "Aren't they awful. I would rather have a non-Communist girl if I were ever to get married!"

On the other hand, I knew a widow who had once been a pious Christian but who now followed her daughter to all Communist social gatherings in the firm belief that there were nicer young men for her daughter to choose from among Communists nowadays than among church-going people. I also came across a number of apostates who, disappointed in the behavior of most

Japanese Christians during the war, were turning toward what they called "communist-humanism."

But as a whole, the Communists and sympathizers of the time—at least those I came to know—seemed to me harmless, powerless, rather uninteresting people. I felt that many of them, with their still largely feudalistic mental habits, were turning communism into just another of their mannerisms, that is, a form of worship, and I felt danger of a kind in that. So I was greatly relieved when the boys stopped going too far into the movement.

Our older boy had been going round with a handsome girl who was a qualified pharmacist, but who wished to be an actress. We had been worried about this, too, because we thought she was not a very steady kind. When she suddenly stopped coming to our house, we were rather pleased, although our son looked depressed. After he had been on a business trip to the north, he came home with his former cheerfulness. He said he had met the most beautiful girl in all Hokkaido. Some time later he announced his engagement to her and went over to her home. This was a few months after Kazuko was married.

We felt dizzy to think of another wedding so soon, but were most pleased with this girl when our boy brought her to Tokyo with him and found a job for her. We did not think her beautiful, as our boy did, but rather a healthy, pleasant-looking young woman, warm-hearted and straight forward. Her large round eyes, slightly curly hair and straight nose appeared to us more European than Japanese. These two young people were really in love with each other and acted like happy lovers of the liberated, free, democratic Japan where young boys and girls worked, studied and played together, walked arm in arm and fell in love quite wisely. I was glad and grateful that our second child had also selected his partner by himself and so wisely too.

The family's only concern was how to get them married and to have them establish a household of their own. Our house was already packed to the breaking point, but we could not tell them to wait until a house or a room could be obtained, for that meant waiting an indefinite time. They each had a job and could support themselves, as long as they hung on to their jobs in the face of the ever-increasing unemployment and as long as they did not get ill and had no children. Well, that was all they could plan and hope for their marriage. As for the housing question, we simply had to make room for them in our house, by squeezing ourselves together just a little more tightly. We had to accept the fact that for contemporary boys and girls, freed from the old family and social restrictions, love had to develop quickly into marriage without any future planning. There was little that the parents, glad or sorry, could do to help or check them.

The wedding was celebrated at the headquarters of the labor union where the marrying couple worked. The bridegroom wore a handsome dark blue suit, a gift from America, remade into a smaller size. The bride was dressed in her best western style suit. They did not care nor could they afford to observe any traditional form. Another pair were married at the same time and many of the union members were present. The gay company cheered the occasion with spirited singing and merry speeches. It was lucky indeed that the grandmother was not there. She could not have stood all the rough unceremoniousness of the marriage ceremony of her oldest grandson, heir to her illustrious family. Coming home, we had a small family party, and enjoyed the delicious cakes and candies I had saved out of the Christmas packages from America.

Our boy and his wife have lived with us ever since. They both go out to work. The grandmother has much greater understanding of the peculiar domestic situation of her granddaughter-in-law than she had of mine at the time of my marriage into her family, because she has now her married granddaughter living with her, and has known the actual problems of a married woman with a professional career. She does not feel quite right about my acting as a friend and not a properly dignified mother-in-law toward my daughter-in-law. But she puts up with it as another of the postwar strangenesses which can not be helped.

Another shock the old lady has had to put up with is the fact that her eldest grandson and the heir to her great family, and a bright Tokyo Imperial University graduate besides, should have married a miner's daughter! The old lady herself had once been considered of too lowly a family to be readily accepted by her august parents-in-law. It had taken her years to acquire a status in her husband's family. But her grandson, according to the new Civil Code, needed no one's consent to his choice of a wife, who thus automatically became a member of the family on her marriage. Moreover, the bride calls her husband by his plain name before everybody and lets him run errands for her to the grocer's and the noodleman's shop!

To me, as well to my husband, our daughter-in-law is a sincere joy. She is fearless, independent, kind-natured and social-minded. In a word, she is a truly democratic woman. Her family, both paternal and maternal, moved out of the main island into Hokkaido in the early years of this century and settled in a mining town in this newly colonized northern island. Her father is a hard-working miner and her mother a cultured, efficient, kind-hearted woman. Both have done their utmost to give their six children the best possible educations. Evidently during the war, they were far better off than my family. The daughter is surprisingly free from all feudalistic inferiority complexes so common with Japanese women, probably because she was brought up in a happy home where simplicity and love, instead of the pretentious feudal family law, governed and also because her home town in Hokkaido is a community of new settlers from the main island, liberated from the main bulk of the ancient traditions of the Japanese people. A Japanese woman of her type is a delightful new discovery to me.

Our younger boy now sings and acts in a company of boys and girls who visit night clubs, factories and hospitals. The earnings of these travelling players are very small, evidently because there are many such troupes competing. It seems a kind of fashion nowadays for young men, unemployed or unwilling to be subjected to mechanical office work, and young women scorning housework and office employment, to form companies of this kind and travel throughout the country. Consequently almost all of these actors are amateurs of mediocre talent.

Our boy has plenty of chances to see girls, but they are without exception, proud, independent, hard-headed girls who have chosen—against the will of their parents or guardians—this difficult path of life, and who will never fall in love with a boy who is not earning even his own living. So our younger boy, now twenty-four, will not marry for some time yet. More than that, we are worried about his staying too long with these amateur actors. He is still the greatest problem for the family.

15. Our Glamor Girl

Our houses became really overcrowded when our two older children married and continued to live with us. Then, to our great alarm, Yasuko, our youngest daughter, began to act wildly.

Neighborhood societies and block offices continued to function for some time after the close of the war, primarily for the distribution of rationed food. But instead of air-raid drills and caring for refugees, they now had to foster a "democratic spirit" among the people. But what was a democratic spirit? The neighborhood talked it over seriously, and decided that it had to do with young people's and women's participation in social life. Thus "young people's cultural meetings," where boys and girls practiced social dancing and English conversation, and held discussions on "democratic subjects," came to be held frequently in our neighborhood.

Yasuko went with her younger brother to these meetings, and particularly to the dancing classes. From the very first lesson she danced beautifully and attracted every boy present. Very soon our doorway became crowded with boys, but our girl could not ask them into the house, because it was so full of people that there was no place to sit down comfortably.

I was sincerely sorry for her because she had been crowded out of the house by her married brother and sister who were too absorbed in their own affairs to think of the discomfort and general neglect their little sister was suffering. With their arrival, she had been pushed away into the corner of a tiny dingy room which she had to share with her grandmother. Naturally she disliked staying at home and got into the habit of sneaking out without telling us where she was going. So whenever I got gifts of clothes from America I gave her the best and most colorful, hoping that she might feel her discomfort compensated by pretty dresses. She was delighted by the lovely American things, but just the same she was restless.

Just as she was advanced to the fifth year of high school, she announced she was not going to school any more. We were dismayed, but I knew scolding would make the matter worse for her, and argued it out with my husband and some other members of the family. I tried to get her interested in either English typing or dress-making—the two most popular postwar occupations for Japanese women. But the first day she went to an English business school several boys asked her for dates, and one of whom took her to a dance hall where she made several more new boy acquaintances.

She was fast turning into a glamor girl. The slim little girl, still with short, straight hair and no paint, was not much to look at, but her long-lashed, almond-shaped eyes twinkled fearlessly, and her merry laughter and spritely repartee was evidently an inexhaustible source of fascination to boys. A glamor girl in postwar Japan, however, did not mean a dainty butterfly feeding on delicacies. At one time Yasuko used to get up at five every morning to stand in line for a full hour in the morning cold, in order to buy a package of cigarettes for her boy friend. One day she came home beaming, hugging "a lovely present" from one of her beaux. "Let me see," I said expectantly. It was a discarded can with a bit of good washing soap in the bottom!

Even on these meagre levels of social enjoyment, our boys and girls always had to struggle for their pocket money, if not for their food and shelter. Temptations were many for them—black-marketeering and gambling being the least harmful of the means they resorted to for earning money. Particularly for my younger girl's sake, I was grateful for the lovely clothes and delicious foods I received from my American friends. Without them I can not imagine what would have become of her, for they enabled me to provide her with luxuries at a time when such things could only be obtained by stealing or prostitution— acts which the chaotic society of the time sadly overlooked. Moreover, these beautiful gifts gave grace to her awakening days when graces of any kind were few and were thoughtlessly trampled upon under want and sordidity.

What worried me most was the lack of proper environment, particularly a healthy home background for the young people's social life. I did not object to the country-wide mania for social dancing, but where could our boys and girls meet each other under normal circumstances? Our neighborhood societies' so-called dance parties were given in the home of one neighbor or another, where young people got together and danced to the gramophone music. Beyond that, there were neither big halls nor money in our neighborhood to conduct truly sociable gath-erings. Our young people soon got tired of dancing on the mat floor of a tiny Japanese room to a squeaky victrola. The more wilful of them turned to dance halls and cabarets which were rising in great numbers throughout the country as one of the most flourishing industries of postwar Japan.

My daughter, after her first visit to a dance hall, expressed great surprise at the scantiness of dress and painted finger-nails and toe-nails of the women there. Evidently the Japanese, who had told their women at the time of the landing of the Occupa-tion forces, to wear long-skirted kimonos and tight obis, and cover their feet with cotton socks, stared at their first sight of the light dress and perfect composure of the Allied women, who began to appear in the streets of Japanese cities the next sum-mer after the Occupation. Soon, however, they reorganized their outlook toward feminine dress and caught up with world level. Japanese women now danced in cabaret halls in sarong-style evening gowns.

My daughter reported· that many of the women in the cab-aret houses were taxi-dancers, and that many of these dancers for hire were war-widows, who had been burnt out or repatri-ated from the Continent. Each had a sad story to tell of how she had been stranded on this growing crust of postwar Tokyo—a series of tragic, wasteful quarrels with her parents-in-law, accounts of hellish repatriation journeys from a far outpost of the collapsed Japanese Empire, recollections of nights spent penniless, foodless and shivering in the street with her little children, and so on.

The men who frequented these houses were extremely dressy, and the greater part of their conversation was about the selling and buying of clothes and textiles. Evidently clothes offered the biggest field for black-marketeering just then and hoarded textiles and the stocks of kimono and Western dress—men's suits and overcoats in particular—which had been preserved from the air-raids, were now put on sale in great volumes. The Japanese people were sick of all shades of khaki, which they had been made to call "the national defense color," and were putting most of their scanty money into clothes which did not remind them of the hateful war and fallen militarism. It was a pity that the beauty of khaki color, which had been so dearly loved by the "tea culture men" of Japan, and had so enriched the meditative temper of the race in the past, had been totally destroyed by its association with modern warfare.

But this was no time for the contemplation of the subtle, evasive beauty of khaki color. A shirt with holes in it was obtainable only in exchange for a huge pile of money, or for sheer love, or plain stealing. "At these cabaret houses," my daughter commented, "people look at clothes first and then at faces."

These dandified black-marketeers, who were the best patrons of the cabaret houses, were mostly young men in their twenties and early thirties. Men over forty rarely succeeded in catching up with the reckless *après la guerre* spirit. Some were teen-age boys, already with records of repeated arrests and imprisonments. Those who were particularly well-dressed and showed a slightly peculiar accent in their spoken Japanese were Koreans, Formosans and Chinese, who were cleverer than Japanese nationals in the economic anarchy of the country of the time. These cabarets were "off-limits" to the Occupation personnel.

My daughter once told me of "a sweet, dimpled little girl called Saye-chan," who appeared at a cabaret with a young man in handsome American clothes, whose bright color and oversizedness gave him an apish look. Saye-chan's family lived in a corner of a chicken coop, and although there were no more chickens in the coop because feeds were so expensive and moreover some other people besides her family had to live there, the place still smelled of chickens, which Saye-chan could not bear. She just wanted to wear clean clothes and sleep in a clean room. So she ran away from her family and was picked up by this young man, who gave her all that she wanted. She wanted to buy some of the delicious-looking foods and lovely clothes which were displayed in such abundance in the shop-windows along the streets. She also thought she had a right to wear, once in a while, a pair of brand new stockings which had no holes and which were a *real* pair, the right and the left exactly the same color and size!

Saye-chan was a beautiful dancer and was loved by everybody in the house, but after a week of wild gaiety she abruptly disappeared. Her companion, a boy of nineteen, had been arrested for a third time for trading in American dollars and goods.

The story saddened me most bitterly. I shuddered at the thought of innocent young people so ruthlessly exposed to the crimes and abandonment of a defeated nation, and sincerely wished for the quick recovery of decent homes where our children could be properly taken care of. Our government was strangely slow in helping the people to rebuild their houses, while allowing the fast rise of any number of amusement houses, cabarets, restaurants and tea-houses, which thrived the more because of the lack of normal home life for the people.

I listened with a mixture of dismay and relief when Yasuko confided in me that she was in love with a boy in our neighborhood and wanted to marry him. I was dismayed because she was so young—just eighteen—and also because I had no money whatsoever for her marriage. But I was glad in a way, because her marriage would end the family's anxiety lest she get into trouble. The boy she wanted to marry seemed to be a reliable young man, although he was not completely free from the general restlessness and rashness that marked the young people of postwar Japan. He was still a student, his service in the navy during the war having delayed his going through college. But he had a house of his own and some other possessions left by his late father, and he was just as anxious to marry her.

I could not tell her to wait, to stay home where she had no place even to sit comfortably now that a baby had been born to her elder sister, and had become the centre of our family life. So, only five months after our older boy got married, we celebrated another wedding. The bride's trousseau consisted exclusively of American gifts, for I did not have a cent left in my savings-account after financing the two previous family weddings, and the hospital expenses for the grandmother who had just had an operation. My husband's teaching salaries were nearly always in arrears, due to the financial troubles of the colleges where he taught, and besides, they were the slowest of all salaries to be adjusted to the mounting prices. We could not buy a single piece of furniture for her, but the bridegroom and his mother were well satisfied, because at that time even a single bundle of clothes was considered a goodly bridal outfit. They were impressed by the abundance of pretty American dresses she possessed, and neither they nor any one else seemed to notice that these clothes did not fit the slim little girl. Remaking any one of them into a smaller size would cost hundreds or even thousands of yen, for sewing machines were even rarer than proper looking houses in Tokyo, and sewing thread was another grave problem. So people did not mind the size at all so long as clothes stayed on one's back, and if these were good-looking, they were unconditionally fascinated.

The wedding had also to be as simple as possible. A small feast was held at the bridegroom's home, where close relatives on both sides met and exchanged winecups of goodwill. Yasuko wore a white frilled blouse and red tweed skirt, both gifts from the Wellesley Overseas Committee, and a pink sweater an American friend of mine had got for her, together with a pair of shoes and nylon stockings. She was overjoyed with these fineries, most of which were brand new or just as good. For the first time in her life she put on things newly bought to her size, and was taken to the bridegroom's house. Her grandmother wept to see her pretty little granddaughter marry in such an abrupt manner.

We all hoped that our glamor girl would have a happy marriage. When she had a baby girl, whom her husband named after me, she thought she was the happiest woman in the world. Then, shortly after finishing college, her husband developed pleurisy. It was most unexpected of this big, strong-looking boy, unless we attributed it to the hard life he had undergone while in the navy. From the cases of our two sons-in-law we were inclined to conclude that our ex-soldiers, even when coming home in apparent health, had slowly succumbed to the effect of the harsh military life, becoming apparent only some years later.

Yasuko's husband was laid up in bed for a few months, and even after recovering he was without a job for a long time. Out of sheer financial necessity, my daughter tried the examinations for a waitress's position in a cabaret, reputed to be the most elite and most expensive one in Tokyo. She passed and has worked there ever since. Her mother-in-law, the sweetest and most patient woman I have ever known, takes care of her baby now.

But trouble has arisen with her husband. We were amazed when, on the old feudal claim that the wife's money belonged to the husband, he put her earnings in his own post-office savings-accounts or used them as he pleased. My daughter, who now shoulders the greater part of her husband's family budget, which includes the partial support of his mother, younger brother and sister, has to ask her husband's permission to use her own money for herself or her baby. He has a good sense of money, and is loving to his wife in his own way. But he is a downright despot of the old feudal type, who denies the personality of his wife or any other member of his family to such an extent that he never feels obliged to keep his word to any of them. His will, however changeable, is law to the family. His mother, a patient, placid woman, serves her son as the head of the family in the same way as she once served her august lord, his father. He has recently found a job, but my daughter says she will continue to work and keep her independence.

This son-in-law of mine is another new discovery to me. Evidently his past naval training and his family heritages from his despotic father have kept him as he is. Neither college education—in fact, he hardly ever attended the classes—payment of tuition and attendance at the term examinations being enough to get a diploma in those days of confusion—nor the loud postwar propaganda for "democracy" and "basic human rights" has given a streak of modern humanism to his outlook on life. I wonder if the country still abounds in young men of his type.

Some people criticize my family for allowing our girl to work in such a place, and none of us is very happy about her way of earning money. But in present-day Japan, where practically every man and woman, whether married or not, has to work for a living, where the mother has to share amply in the material support of the children, and where attractive women are beset with temptations of all kinds, I rather think that a cabaret waitress is a fit occupation for my pretty, witty, spritely daughter. It is sad that mixed society, which is a part of the normal daily life of the people of the Western countries, is still a commercialized affair in this country. The destruction of home life by the war, and the peculiar localization of money in the postwar national economy have even accelerated this deplorable tendency, and young women of social charm are in great demand as public entertainers.

Unlike the traditional *geisha* girls, whose expensive professional training used to be the principal basis for the heavy exploitation subsequently laid on them by the investors, these new-type entertainers do not need much training and consequently are not subjected to bitter exploitation. A cabaret waitress's only requirements are a pleasant manner in social dancing, conversation and offering refreshments. Moreover, high-class cabarets in Tokyo have greatly changed since the early Occupation days. Black-marketeering having practically disappeared, petty profit-mongers have largely dropped out of sight. They have been superseded by young men of war-rich families, popular millionaire writers and artists, and business men entertaining each other in this gratifying postwar manner for the purpose of smoothing out their knotty business transactions. With the removal of the "off limits" regulations, men of the Allied countries have noticeably crowded out the lean-pursed Japanese patrons. It is a discouraging fact but my younger daughter, working from seven to eleven every evening, is by far the biggest money-earner in our family circle.

She is the kind of woman who cannot and will not quietly

succumb to the joyless drudgery of a poor Japanese housewife. She demands gaiety and graciousness of life, and her present occupation gives her some degree of satisfaction and steadies her against sweeping temptations. However, the commercialization and capitalization of feminine charm has many risks, and my daughter is hard-headed enough to appreciate the security of married life in contrast to the terrible money-consciousness of her business world. It is urgently hoped that this unhealthy social phenomenon of a very limited group of people controlling the greater part of the nation's money and showering pretty girls with thousand-yen bills, will not last long. And I know, and my girl knows, that she must be prepared for the change.

Part Five

DEMOCRACY IN JAPAN

✦✦✦✦✦✦✦✦✦✦✦✦✦✦✦✦✦✦✦✦✦✦✦✦✦✦

16. The Liberation of Women

The greatest democratic change that has come to postwar Japan, as far as I can see, is the liberation of women. The national bankruptcy and the subsequent social and economic chaos called forth women's cooperation for the rehabilitation efforts. Men, in their desperate need, did not even mind if women led them. The Occupation government sanctioned all the feminist chances and pushed Japanese women several steps further up the ladder toward emancipation.

The new National Constitution gave women equal rights with men in all fields of our national life. The new Civil Code freed them to a large extent from feudal family laws. The enormous number of women employed in the offices of the General Occupation Headquarters and other Occupation offices were, by the Basic Labor Law, paid on an absolutely equal basis with men, which was an unheard-of thing in prewar Japan, and which made these women workers a big power in our postwar economy. Both government and private offices have followed the Occupation examples in the treatment of their women employees.

Japanese women of all classes, whether married or unmarried, have to work now, and women have jobs in more varied fields than men and find it far pleasanter to work with men now than in the old days. The American ladies-first custom is followed everywhere by foreign men, and for the first time Japanese men have come to understand that to be courteous and friendly toward women is neither a detriment to masculine dignity or to feminine chastity. By the Occupation Army's orders, even special cars have been reserved for women in rush-hour trains in big cities and women ride like an old-time royal cortege instead of being brushed aside rudely by men. Western feminism encouraged Japanese offices and firms to hire English-speaking women at high pay to deal with the Occupation authorities and with foreign buyers. Some commercial firms show off their charming women presidents and directors. An attractive woman with some ability to speak English often may command a top-ranking salary.

The abnormal boom of entertainment industries, in the midst of the general business depression, is even turning the table completely. Night clubs, dance halls, tea-rooms and restaurants demand endless numbers of women workers, with the result that many totally or partially unemployed husbands cook and wash and take care of the children at home while their gayly dressed wives go out to earn money. As a natural by-product, designers, dressmakers and beauty specialists, most of whom are women, have big businesses, for the younger generation of Japanese women have completely taken to the Western mode of dress which, with its enormous consumption rate, demands a large business setup, unlike the durable, old kimono business. Magazines about fashion and handicraft are also a prosperous branch of this newly-risen "mode" industry and some women, including a cousin of mine, have been very successful in this line.

This cousin is a young, handsome woman who is the president of a publishing firm. My first acquaintance with her was when she was a little girl, the eldest of three orphans whose father had just died of tuberculosis and left his family in desperate poverty. The widow and children were assisted by their better-off relatives, particularly by my paternal aunt and her son who then had plenty to spare for poor relatives and friends. The oldest girl began to work as soon as she finished high school, first in a publishing house, and then in a dressmaker's shop. When the war ended and every one was absorbed in the problems of rehabilitation, she borrowed capital to start a woman's magazine about new modes of living and fashions, based on ingenuity, simplicity and good taste practicable for the limited resources of postwar Japanese life. The magazine has sold well and she has since turned her business into a corporation with some twenty employees including her mother and two sisters. Besides the magazine, she now publishes books on art, handicraft, dress-styles and interior decoration, all of a very practical nature and charming quality.

She has recently built a house according to her own ideas, which incorporates the best features of Japanese and Western houses, and is so constructed that any spot and corner of it may be photographed and put in her magazine in no time. For dress she blends, with astonishing effects, the Chinese and Western style and she herself models for her designs. She has no interest in Japanese kimonos like the rest of our young women. "I capitalize on my daily life," she says, "because I have nothing else to run a business by." She has recently married off one of her younger sisters to one of her office boys, and says that she will now capitalize on marriage and child-raising questions. She is hardly thirty yet, and unmarried. All our relatives agree that she is the only up and coming member of our family circle.

It is true that the Occupation's enthusiastic, sweeping reforms have sometimes got the present "democracy in Japan" criticized as somewhat "prefabricated." But so far as women's liberation is concerned, the democratization has struck root deeply into the earth, for the material has long been ready and ripe for the transformation. Some people may say that this is true only of upper and middle class women in big cities and I am inclined to agree. But by "women's liberation" I mean that they have acquired an equal footing with men in family and social life. No doubt our women are still held in bitter servitude by the general national poverty. The liberation from that is another problem which Japanese women, in cooperation with their men, have yet to work out.

"Why, this is a women's paradise!" some Japanese men grumble. "How can a man marry nowadays and be sucked and chewed to the last drop of blood by those red-lipped, snaky-haired harpies?" Circumspect young men stay unmarried and put whatever money they can save out of their meagre salaries into bank accounts.

That modesty and sweet naïveté, once noted in Japanese women of all ages, have nearly completely disappeared, and in postwar Japan girls have become far more realistic and aggressive bargain-drivers than boys. All of which worries parents of nice boys more than parents of pretty girls. A young man of good health, good family and an Imperial University education, who served during the war as a paymaster lieutenant or language officer, and now has a position in the Government Treasury or in one of the concerns reorganized but still savoring of the old *zaibatsu* power, is a rare treasure indeed, preserved nearly intact from the bourgeois culture of prewar Japan. But these nice boys do not know how to see through the wiles of the war-impoverished, aggressive-mannered girls now filling offices everywhere.

I know several instances of a young man of such perfection falling in love with a girl working in the same office, several years older than the boy in one case, and of an extremely domineering type in another. The parents could not, in the midst of their happy daydreams about their future daughter-in-law, bear to have their precious boys stolen by such "dirty girls." They tried to force on the boys arranged marriages in the old style, only to meet with a definite refusal and a declaration of independence. They yielded in one case, sighed, and with a sad bitterness in their hearts, made permanent arrangements for their family graves with the money the father had intended to give the boy. As far as I know, these marriages, however, have proved quite successful, if judged from the standpoint of the young people themselves.

Girls are much more hard-headed. Their business experience has taught them independence and not to fall in love with a man without money enough to let his wife live in decent style. Very few nice young Japanese males have incomes large enough to support their wives properly. In contrast, the courteous or gallant manners of Occupation men and the breath-takingly, marvellous things they possess have become absolutely irresistible to many Japanese girls. Many parents consider even temporary connections with foreign men to be better for their daughters than the stark poverty and semi-starvation of the average Japanese housewife. In a country where prostitution is conducted in broad daylight on populous city streets, no one asks whether a marriage is national, international, temporary or permanent, or not a marriage at all. Women are now complete mistresses of their circumstances, hard-pressed and precarious as these circumstances may be.

Naturally, divorce has become a very common phenomenon —divorce initiated not by the husband or parents-in-law, as was the traditional way, but by the wife. It seems that Japanese men, long spoiled by the enormous privileges awarded them over their women by our peculiar feudal system, find themselves far more helpless and incompetent than their women under present conditions.

Men of the upper classes present the worst case of all. Stripped of their inherited formalism, wealth and servants, they now appear to be the most downcast creatures on earth, not knowing how to keep themselves alive, in countless cases, except by becoming parasites on their wives' resourcefulness. These wives sometimes commit suicide, but many of them have become business women, working in Occupation offices, or running gift shops where they sell their heirlooms, and bar-rooms where they attract moneyed plebeians by their aristocratic glamor. Ex-Baroness K, my former neighbor, is now managing a grocery shop in a seaside town. She herself, with the help of her husband and surviving son, buys and carries her goods from the wholesale stores in Tokyo. Many of these businesses have failed owing to the inexperience and incompetence of the lady-managers. On the other hand, many women with patience and hard labor are courageously fighting against all odds and building up sound careers and economic independence for themselves. There are also some who resort to quicker ways of making money. But when the wife brings home money and food, the parasite husband seldom asks how she got it. He has become a burden which his wife may cast off at her own will. So divorces of this nature have become particularly numerous among the upper-class families. But through all the strata of our social life, women's long-suppressed discontent toward the tyrannical laws of our family system has finally found opportunity to express itself and many brave women, in the name of freedom and independence, or for the sake of free love, are divorcing their husbands.

Several such cases have occurred among my close acquaintances. A niece of mine, soon after the close of the war, got away from her "old-fashioned" husband and his feudalistic family traditions, took a job in a commercial firm, fell in love with a boy of leftish sympathies, and is remarried very happily now. The daughter of a friend of mine got a divorce because her husband insisted on knowing exactly how she spent the money she earned by giving piano lessons. She preferred being a good pianist for her own sake to being a good book-keeper for her husband.

A girl I taught at a high school was married to a younger brother of a marquis, who even in this war-crushed age could not outgrow the idea that the world was made for him. He only thought of being well-fed and comfortable himself and never held himself responsible for the livelihood of his wife and children. When they had sold all they could, his wife said, "What can we live on now?" The husband answered very calmly, "*You* can work and earn money."

"Yes, I will work and earn money, and feed my children but not *you*," his wife said, and with her two children, she walked out of her husband's house. She is now a partner in a dressmaking business well-favored by Allied ladies, works 16 hours a day and keeps up a cozy, single-room home for her children. "I am incomparably happier now, and so are my children," she says.

For unmarried girls of the former well-to-do classes, now

beset with economic difficulties and family troubles, religious life apparently has a strong appeal. Quite a number of young women, even within my limited knowledge, have sold the beautiful kimonos their parents so painstakingly preserved for them from the air-raids, made up goodly dowries from the sales, and entered Roman Catholic convents. The Catholic nuns form a strong social force the world over, and their influence has been great on the women of postwar Japan. It will add much to the strengthening of Japanese women's social power.

Beyond doubt Japanese women have gained much freedom from the war and the Occupation. Freedom, however, is a thing not to be given but to be earned. And in the case of our women, the price has been dear. The sudden loss of all material resources and the consequent shattering of all social and family formalities has meant the total removal of both protection and fetters for them. It is like being thrown overboard. You are perfectly free to struggle for your life, or sink underwater. Heroic efforts are made everywhere, but unfortunately prostitution has been resorted to frequently. It must be noted, however, that even prostitution is freely chosen now, unlike the prewar days when girls were commonly sold into this profession by their hard-pressed parents.

The freedom awarded to Japanese women today is of the most elementary kind—the freedom for self-defense and survival. It is only after successful survival that their higher power will be liberated. At any rate, a slow but steady progress is being made, and they will never allow themselves to go back to their old servitude, no matter what reactionary setbacks may occur.

We often complain about our past days of comfort and I do sometimes miss the graciousness of life some of my relatives enjoyed in their prewar prosperity. But one good thing that I find in our general impoverishment today is that we have completely outgrown our feudalistic, petty-bourgeois complexes. We now frankly admit that we all belong to the proletarian masses of this proletarian nation, and find a wide range of subjects on which we can talk and sympathize with each other on a sincerely equal basis.

The change is most clearly seen in our husky, independent children. When I was a girl, my generation of boys and girls in our family circle, particularly on my mother's side, were all expected to go to college and university, and most of us did go, all the expenses being paid by the parents. We were terribly snobbish, observing the feudal law of primogeniture and admiring the display of high society. We despised labor and money-earning. But our children are quite different. First of all they do not expect much material support from their parents. Neither do they hold their parents in such authority and reverence as we as children were made to do. They have learned through experience that their individual worth and ability is the primary basis of their life. For them the "ancient family," seen through their impoverished parents' eyes, has lost its meaning. They know that if they demand the privilege of going to college, they must work for it themselves. Some of them must work even through high school. An education for them is a thing to earn and not to be given or forced on them by their parents. So they talk about money and money-earning as a plain matter of course and take the subject as an issue common to all the Japanese people.

My family circle represents a large section of the present-day Japanese people, the bulk of the prewar middle class. So, the tendencies seen in the younger generation in my family must be common to many other children of Japan. As they grow up, I hope their independent, democratic spirit will also grow and bring about happy changes in the social life of our people.

17. The Story of a Revolt

I came to know Ayako the year after the close of the war. She was still wearing a patched mompé overall, but her tall, straight figure and dark quiet eyes instantly fascinated me. I saw her for the first time when she came to my house on some errand from Mrs. Yamada, who was then president of the neighborhood society to which my family had belonged since we had been burnt out and moved into this leftover house. At that time Mrs. Yamada had several assistants for her business and Ayako was one of them.

"Where did you get that charming assistant of yours?" I asked one day when I met my busy neighbor on a neighboring electric line. "You mean that viscountess? I just bumped into her and picked her up," she said.

Mrs. Yamada was an amateur black-marketeer, flying from one rosy promise to another like a busy bee. She met all sorts of people and handled all sorts of things. She had once brought home a war-orphan, one of the shoeblacks of the street, but the boy ran away after a week or so. But how did she happen to pick up an ex-viscountess? I was curious.

We were so desperately occupied at this time with our daily livelihood that we never paid or received social calls, but after a few chance meetings on the street and in tramcars with Mrs. Yamada, I gathered from her the story of this heroic young woman.

Ayako's father was a well-known engineer and high government official. She was married, soon after finishing high school, to a naval lieutenant and heir to a viscount of an old daimyo lineage. Shortly after her marriage her mother died, and some time later her father was killed in a plane crash in Manchuria. In the last air-raid on Tokyo, both her parental home and the home of her parents-in-law where she lived during her husband's absence on the battlefront, were burnt down. Then the report of her husband's death was brought to her eight months after he was killed in the South Pacific.

She now lived with her weeping, wailing parents-in-law in their half-burnt warehouse. She carried home heavy loads of foodstuffs from farmers, or stood three hours in a line to buy a little food, and cooked the precious acquisitions with embers gathered from the charred beams and pillars of the vanished mansion. She cleared away part of the ashes and raised vegetables there by carrying the nightsoil of the family to the furrows. She lived with her parents-in-law and worked hard for them simply because she had nowhere to go, and also because the honorable viscount and viscountess, having no more children left except a married daughter, and no more servants to wait on them, depended entirely on their daughter-in-law. They called "Ayako!" "Ayako!" a hundred times a day.

After the memorial service for the first anniversary of her husband's death, the honorable parents-in-law announced the marriage they had arranged for Ayako. They had adopted a relative of theirs as their heir and Ayako was to marry this man, an ex-army officer. "It is your duty," her parents-in-law remonstrated, "to remarry, have children and have them revenge your first husband and our only son, as well as our country." She could not bear any more war-talk. She revolted and fled to her sister, the only remaining member of her family.

This elder sister of hers was one of those capable, unscrupulous, pretty women who blossomed in the economic, social and moral anarchy following the close of the war. In partnership with a number of her women friends, she owned a curio shop in a lane adjacent to the fast-reviving, most fashionable boulevard of Tokyo. There many ex-peeresses and ex-zaibatsu ladies brought their jewelry, silks, lacquerware and china pieces, bearing their proud family crests, to be sold. The shop looked like a heraldric museum.

Ayako sometimes worked in the shop, but she was, according to the comments of her energetic, ambitious sister, too slow and too undiplomatic, despite her good looks, and therefore altogether unfit for a saleswoman of that kind. So she stayed home most of the time and acted as housekeeper for her busy sister, who nearly everyday went out early in the afternoon and came home after midnight, carrying butter, powdered milk, chocolate, coffee and other delicious and nourishing American foods for her delicate, pale-faced boy and for the rest of the family.

One night Ayako overheard her sister quarreling with her husband, remonstrating that these American foods were absolutely necessary for her invalid boy, and that she had got them in exchange for her spare kimonos, and nothing else.

Ayako liked her generous, kind-hearted brother-in-law, but she had noticed that recently he had become somewhat too attentive to her. One afternoon he asked her to take a walk with him. Although she did not like the idea much, she consented and went out to the Boulevard Ginza. Just as they were walking into a tea-room, a shining, pearl-colored car drew up to the curb a little distance ahead and a man in civilian clothes got out and held the door for the woman who followed him—a handsome, black-haired woman in dark green. Ayako at once remembered the beautiful green suit her sister had shown her a few days before, saying that she had got it in exchange for her orchid-colored wedding robe.

The next moment the woman stood up on the pavement, face in face with her husband! On finding Ayako with him, the sister's face instantly relaxed a little and in perfect dignity and composure she passed on without even a side glance. She walked straight into a store, which was "off limits to Japanese nationals," followed by the unsuspecting foreign gentleman. Ayako looked at the beautiful and abundant American goods displayed in the show-windows of the store, and felt as if her sister had vanished into a dreamland.

That night her sister and brother-in-law had a big quarrel and the next morning Ayako left their home for good. She had no place to go to, so she sat in a corner of a big railway station, holding her bundle of clothes on her lap. Like the rest of the Japanese people, she had acquired this habit of tightly clutching her possessions against the world, infested with thieves and pick-pockets. Darkness was gathering over the ruined, hungry city.

"You want a home." A woman suddenly spoke, standing in front of her. "Your face tells it. Come with me, I need an assistant."

Ayako by now had become accustomed to abrupt turns of life. She looked very quietly at the friendly stranger in tight trousers and rubber boots. She liked the woman's kindly face and clear, softly-modulated voice, which told her that this roughly-dressed worker belonged to the educated class. So with sincere gratefulness and willingness she accepted the invitation.

This was how Lady Ayako was picked up by Mrs. Yamada and became her business assistant.

18. New Adjustments

Mrs. Yamada's husband was a painter, nearly seventy years old, of truly lovely flowers and birds. He presented these exquisite pictures to his friends or kept them in his atelier and showed them to interested visitors. He never sold any, as if fearing that the least thought of money would instantly kill off the soul of the flower he had caught with his brush. Evidently all through the war and postwar years he did practically nothing but paint flowers and birds.

All day long he sat in his atelier in the midst of rolls of mulberry paper and glazed silk, boxes upon boxes of paints and several dozen bamboo-handled brushes, ranging from the size of lamp chimneys to the finest knitting needles. Leaning against the walls of the room stood his pictures, each carefully covered with cotton cloth.

I visited his atelier only once, but I shall never forget that experience. I went to see Mrs. Yamada and ask her to get just a small amount of rice for my family. Not finding her, I peeped through an opening between the sliding screens, and gave a cry of joy as I caught a glimpse of a cluster of purple-blue *gaku* flowers. Suddenly I remembered that there were such things as flowers and beautiful pictures in this world. I had had no time to think of them these past several years, since the sight and odor of omnipresent rubbish and filth had so debased my senses.

The gray-bearded artist came out gently smiling and asked me to come in. He took the coverings off one picture after another. A cascade of forsythia sprays tumbled out, loaded with the pearly gold of an early spring sun. A large purple flower of the tree peony tossed its glorious head the moment before it was to crumble away into a fragrant, silky pile of shedded petals. Here was a shaded pond trimmed with dead, tattered lotus plants, where a king-fisher sat, a ball of emerald-green with a bright red streak on the beak, set against the gray, broken shapes of winter.

"It is strange," the old artist said quietly, "but the world looks lovelier than ever to me. It may be because I am old now and leaving this life very soon, or it may be that the miseries and horrors of war are now set off in more intense contrast to the beautiful things of this life." He sighed, and there were glistening tears in his sunken eyes.

The Yamadas once had a modest amount of property on which they lived frugally and peacefully, but the postwar inflation completely uprooted them. In order to keep themselves going, Mrs. Yamada tried her hand at many things—farm work, street vending, assisting in a beauty parlor, etc., etc.

In the early postwar years when the country had not yet started producing general commodities, and when the value of paper money depreciated fast, the people who had barely preserved their goods from the air-raids found it necessary to liquidate them quickly. The black market for this kind of goods was conducted on a system of minutely ramifying feelers which groped in the dark until any one of them picked up the best possible bargain. In other words, it required many people to run about and relay the information and transaction between the original supplier and the final buyer. There were hardly any telephones working among the Japanese inhabitants of Tokyo at that time, and a letter took a week to get from one end of the city to the other, if not further delayed at the censorship office with whatever secret message it contained for all to see. So all messages had to be carried personally and orally and at the quickest possible speed through the terrific traffic jams.

A vast volume of black-marketing thus flourished in the abnormal economic condition of the country, and nearly everybody got involved in it, ranging from huge deals in embezzled public commodities to half a dozen pencils for school children. Evidently Mrs. Yamada made an excellent broker because of her indefatigable energy, unwavering courage and pleasant sociability, and for a time at least, she made a thriving business out of it. At that time, besides Ayako, she had her own brother, his wife, and two student boarders living with her. They all helped her with her business, and for emergency needs she could get any number of young men in the neighborhood, including my two boys, who were all very anxious to earn pocket money. It seems, however, that Ayako mostly took the part of housekeeper for the busy black-marketeers and the shy, old artist. When occasionally she too was called to business, the artist himself kept the house for the rest of the family. He would rather scrub in the kitchen than handle money.

I know nothing personally about the criminal black-marketeering of the time, but the brokers and speculators on the homely scale of Mrs. Yamada seemed to me interesting and enviable people, because they formed an active, hopeful minority in the midst of subdued, bewildered people. Mrs. Yamada and her assistants ran about from morning till late at night, looking as radiant and as important as if they were swimming and riding on rainbow-colored bubbles. Their sole aim was to earn enough money so that they could eat good rice and occasional delicacies, and not have to subsist day in and day out for five weeks at a stretch on nothing but the government-rationed musty, bitter-tasting corn flour with nothing, not even enough salt, to go with it. If in addition to rice and some fat, Mrs.

Yamada got just a little more money so that she might supply her husband with paints and brushes, it was all the reward she wanted from her frantic business life. And I know that for a woman past fifty, without special technical training, this was the only way, in these days, that she could keep herself and her family alive.

19. Women and Kimonos

Japan, once one of the biggest weaving countries of the world, had not yet reconstructed its textile industry. People who had saved anything from the air-raids had been forced to live "bamboo sprout fashion," selling off their possessions one after another as young bamboo shoots quickly shed their sheathing leaves. Thus kimono dealers were very busy people.

Mrs. Yamada had explained to me that Japanese kimonos of good, solid silk, easily adjustable to any individual size, and practically free from the tyranny of fashion, had a permanence and a universality which made them far more dependable as currency than the inflated paper money. Western clothes were also in good circulation, although fashion controlled their prices to a great extent. Men's suits, trousers and overcoats were easily disposed of, and even women's thin, faded dresses had come to sell quite well, owing to the universal adoption of Western dress by young Japanese women. Good cottons and woolens were considered as solid financially as gold bullion.

Orders for bridal robes with colors and family crests designated were eagerly sought after. Fond parents dressed up their daughters more gorgeously than ever now that good kimonos were obtainable only at fabulously high cost.

One day Mrs. Yamada brought out two ceremonial kimonos, one magenta-colored and the other a green and gold brocade, and asked Ayako to take them to a certain kimono dealer. These ceremonial kimonos, Mrs. Yamada explained, bore family crests of three fan-shaped weights arranged in a circle, exactly the kind her boss had been looking for. A wealthy country family who had this rather rare figure for their family crest were collecting costly kimonos for their daughter's wedding trousseau. These were kimonos of the best kind, said Mrs. Yamada, obtained, after much searching, from the wardrobe of a certain ex-titled lady, and the family crests being designated by order, they called for much higher prices than otherwise. The magenta one, worn only once, would sell for 11,500 yen and the green and gold brocade, completely new, 16,000 yen. Out of these sums Mrs. Yamada would like to have 12% for commission.

Ayako felt a strange nervousness about having charge of such costly merchandise. Then suddenly she was caught by painful nostalgia for the days when she herself had possessed lovely things, and enjoyed the solid security of parental care— days now abruptly and irretrievably vanished. Lovely kimonos were once a matter of course to her. She used to have a ceremonial kimono just like this magenta-colored one, only a shade lighter, with sprays of plum flowers painted and embroidered all over in opalescent pinks, purples and gold. She had never worn it. It was put away in the second drawer of the first paulownia chest, together with the blue ceremonial kimono with figures of pale yellow and green dandelions, and the lavender-colored under-kimono to go with either the magenta or the blue robe. She could clearly see in her mind that beautiful chest, all the five drawers filled with ceremonial kimonos just as rich and colorful as these two pieces she was going to take on Mrs. Yamada's errand. If one such piece sold for more than 10,000 yen, how many millions had she lost overnight!

With the valuable merchandise carefully tied up in a bundle under her arm, she started on her trip. She changed car lines several times and came to the northeastern edge of the city. This, like many other parts of Tokyo, was a trackless expanse of war-wreckage, with tiny shacks, hardly bigger than a match box, scattered over it at random. After getting lost several times in the maze of footpaths leading to all directions, she finally found the house she was looking for.

It was a tiny house like the rest, for there were government regulations just then about the size of new houses, but it was an extremely pretty one, with even a garden and a bamboo fence around it. The well-trimmed hedge of sweet daphne was abloom in intoxicating fragrance. The stone lantern in the garden was screened by a slim maple tree ready to burst into tender buds, and trimmed at the base with curly ferns and glossy *tsuwabuki* leaves. The whole composition was so small and neat that Ayako thought she could almost pick up the house and garden in her palm and fondle it as if it were a sparkling gem. In fact, in postwar Tokyo, a house was longed for far more than heaps of jewels. It was the sincerest desire and

· 185 ·

fondest dream of every Japanese to live just once more in a proper house. To Ayako, the cottage looked like a gracious apparition, floating momentarily in the rubbishy world. What blessed people out of a fairy tale lived in such a house as this? she wondered.

Although built in pure, traditional Japanese style, the cottage had one marked postwar feature. The sliding door of the front entrance was locked tight, with a door bell for a caller to press. When a young woman came out in answer to the bell, guest and hostess looked at each other in dumbfounded surprise for a moment and then gave cries of joy.

"Why, Lady Ayako!" the hostess spoke first. "How did you know I was living here?" In a mixture of surprise, joy and mystification, Ayako's former housemaid eyed her ex-mistress.

Ayako was rather self-conscious of her shabby, worn-out dress, and of the nature of the errand she had been sent on. But soon she got over it and sincerely congratulated her ex-servant on her postwar prosperity. She admired everything—her beautiful house, the lovely kimono Ohisa wore, and the costly furniture she had collected.

The flattered girl, in a very ceremonious manner, introduced her former mistress to her sister-in-law, who cast puzzled, inquisitive glances at this worn-looking girl in patched clothes. Ohisa explained that she was living with her brother and his family, that her brother and she were jointly conducting a kimono brokerage business. They had many good connections with big country families which had grown rich during the war and were buying up quantities of kimonos and jewelry from impoverished city people. Their business was booming wonderfully.

Ohisa opened the bundle Ayako had brought, inspected the kimonos with the air of a professional and said that these were excellent acquisitions, and that Mrs. Yamada was a wonderful sub-broker who had never disappointed them. The superior air this kimono-woman assumed toward Mrs. Yamada as her sub-broker pricked Ayako with a painful sense of humiliation about her present position.

"It's inexcusable!" Ohisa exclaimed almost in a hysterical fit when Ayako told that all her marriage trousseau had been lost. "If you had saved them, we could have helped you to get tens of millions of yen out of them honestly. It's criminal!" She was indignant.

It was only five years before that Ohisa, as a poor country girl obliged to earn money to help her hard-pressed father, came to work in Ayako's parental home. She was bright, clever and hard-working. She had almost no clothes then and was happy to get the young mistress's discarded kimonos. She was overjoyed when Ayako gave her a Western dress which had grown too small for her. Ohisa wanted to go out in it so badly that Ayako also gave her a good pair of shoes from her handsome collection, although her mother disapproved. The shoes hurt her feet terribly but the young country girl was transported with joy and pride at this complete modernization of her dress. How simple and how easily pleased she was then!

Ayako felt guilty at showing the poor housemaid the rich trousseau her parents were preparing for her. But after working in her home for a year or so, Ohisa went back home because she had to help her father in the field since her brother had been called to military service. Soon after Ayako married and her mother was taken ill.

The last days of the war broke off all lines of communication and people lost track of each other, resulting in the most tragic rending of family ties and friendships. Now, relatives and friends, if still alive after the awful tribulations, were picking up the broken threads of their former connections, sometimes in the most unexpected tragi-comic reunions.

With suppressed giggles Ohisa told the story of ex-Baron Shiba, a cousin of Ayako's mother, in whose household Ohisa's brother formerly worked and through whose introduction Ohisa came to serve in Ayako's parental home. One day, when Ohisa's brother went to a public bath, the nearest one from his house, he saw a head floating in the pool, gray-haired with a moustache of the same shade, handsomely curled up at both ends. That moustache at once reminded him of his former master Lord Shiba. Why, it was the head of Lord Shiba himself! The surprised ex-servant jumped out of the pool and sat on the tiled floor outside the pool, completely nude, of course, but in the most ceremonious fashion and bowed low, saying, "My lord, at your service, your humble servant Yakichi."

The ex-nobleman shyly smiled, so Ohisa recounted, and said simply, "Never mind, I am a common man now." He was so shy that he stayed in the pool as long as he could bear the heat. He got so red that he looked like a boiled octopus!

In the midst of the fit of laughter in which Ayako and Ohisa had been caught, the door bell rang and Ohisa's brother Yakichi came home. He had been on a trip into the country, and the rucksack he carried on his back was stuffed with paper money. He told his wife to take the rucksack to the bank at once and deposit the 570,000 yen contained in it.

Yakichi was very happy to see Ayako and the beautiful ceremonial kimono she had brought from Mrs. Yamada. He was going to make another trip into the country the following day.

"Would you like to live with us and be a partner in our business?" Yakichi asked Ayako.

Ohisa warmly supported her brother's suggestion. Of course no one could be a lady of leisure nowadays, Ohisa said, and since Ayako deserved a better home and a better job than she had at Mrs. Yamada's, they would be happy to provide her with it. Ohisa was extremely self-confident and content about her business.

Ayako was somewhat tempted at first, but decided that she preferred the artist's home to the reckless brokerage and black-marketeering of the nouveaux riches. First of all, she could not take a frantic interest in kimonos as merchandise. It was painful to see lovely things sold off by hard-pressed owners for the sake of tomorrow's bread. She would rather stay with Mrs. Yamada, who had been very good to her and who, despite her brusque, high-spirited practicality, understood the gentleness of life.

When Ayako definitely declined their kind offer, the prosperous kimono dealers were puzzled. "You will come to see us often then," Ohisa said. Yakichi said that ex-Baron and Baroness Shiba were coming to live in the house he was building next door to his own, and proudly showed the spot where several workmen were busy. The burnt-out nobleman and his wife were living just then in a room in a friend's house, not far from there but had been asked to leave since the house had to be sold by the bankrupt owner. Ohisa added that the Baron's young son was coming home shortly from New Guinea.

Though it was still early in the afternoon, Ayako was entertained with a sumptuous dinner—offering a meal at any time of the day or night was a sign of the warmest hospitality among the hungry Japanese people—and was presented with a pongee kimono and a pair of wooden clogs, exactly the kind of presents a servant used to receive from her mistress in the prewar days.

She thought for a moment of going over to see Uncle and Aunt Shiba, but somehow she did not feel very anxious to see them. In her changed state she felt shy at meeting any of her old acquaintances. Moreover, she did not have much time, because she had to get home before dark, for walking alone after dark was never safe for a young woman in any part of Tokyo.

When Ayako left her former housemaid's costly, shiny new house and started back across the desolate plains of Tokyo to Mrs. Yamada's rickety house, she felt peculiarly despondent. She was unselfish enough to be happy about Ohisa's business success, but in the presence of her prosperity and self-confidence, she had felt herself completely belittled, just a poor, penniless, homeless war-widow, drifting among the masses of helpless, shiftless war-refugees. She began to weep and big tears wetted the pongee kimono and wooden clogs, Ohisa's handsome presents, which she carried, carefully wrapped and held in her arm.

She was happy to have that kimono but it was not half so good as the one Ohisa had on. "Well, I used to give her only discarded kimonos when she was my maid," Ayako thought, and clearly saw herself standing at the lower end of the up-turned social scale.

20. Long-Suppressed Voices

Early in the summer of 1947 Mr. Yamada died of apoplexy. It was a Sunday and I was out on a buying trip in the country, so I did not hear of his death until I came home late in the evening. I went to see Mrs. Yamada the following morning. The coffin was placed in the atelier and just a single picture of chrysanthemums was shown over it, all other pictures having been covered up and put away in the corner.

Mrs. Yamada told me that her husband had been working on that painting until the last moment. The luxuriant sprays of wild chrysanthemum flowers emerged out of muffled twilight, showing the graceful contours of their stems and leaves in soft, cloudy green-grays. The bunches of full-blown blossoms, pearly yellow, pale gray and bits of carmine, caught on their myriads of sharp needle-like petals the hovering light of dawn and imbued the misty air with the soft medicinal odor which they exaled. Nebulous and wan at first sight, the host of flowers seemed as if to collect and absorb the opalescent rays of a dewy morning and hold them there in such abundance and intensity that there was an abyss of burning silveriness created, ready to ignite a contemplative soul and free it from the world of matter! I felt sure the old artist had stepped right into that picture— the Heaven of Flowers which his soul had so longed for.

An incense of rare aroma, long treasured in the bottom of Mrs. Yamada's antique chest of drawers, was burnt before the mirage of heavenly flowers. Pale blue smoke rose out of the bronze burner in a wavering gossamer mist and, as each visitor added a fingertipful, it convoluted anew into a filigree of intricate knots and spirals.

"Only yesterday morning," Mrs. Yamada said tearfully, "my husband told me that he had dreamed of our son standing on what seemed to be a wild, pine-covered hillside, veiled in silvery haze, and calling and beckoning us both. 'Our son is dead,' my husband said. Only a few hours later he was gone."

The Yamadas' son had been reported missing in the Philippines, and recently the Demobilization Office had sent confirmation of his death to his parents, together with his "heroic spirit," which was a cube-shaped wooden box containing a piece of paper bearing two Chinese characters "heroic" and "spirit." This was the way our government made up for the unrecoverable remains of more than a million Japanese soldiers who were supposed to have perished in the South Pacific areas. But Mrs. Yamada refused to accept such a government report and indomitably insisted that the boy, like many other unfortunate youth of Japan, was still living somewhere in the tropic wilderness.

Only once had Mrs. Yamada spoken to me about her boy. "He hated war," she said emphatically. "He was just out of Tokyo Imperial University, majoring in economics. He loved to paint, but he chose a more practical career, seeing the hard lot I had as an artist's wife. When war became inevitable, he chose the navy because he thought that in the navy fighting was more or less between machines, and not between human beings. He thought fighting a machine was less cruel than killing fellow humans. But after all, he was dumped on land with the rest of the soldiers in the midst of the battle of Luzon without even proper weapons and food supplies." Mrs. Yamada's eyes shone with pity and indignation. "But I am pretty sure," she added with a hopeful sigh, "he ran away into the mountains instead of making a foolish charge on the enemy. He used to say that, try as he did, he could not hate American boys."

One morning toward the end of that summer we were informed of the sudden passing away of Mrs. Yamada. She had lost her vigor and sociability since her husband's death and for some time she had not been seen around, but I had not realized the end was so near. Then when I went to her house and saw what had happened, I understood how the mother's strength, drawn tight by wilful hope and the rush of daily livelihood, had suddenly snapped.

Mrs. Yamada's brother showed me some sheets of old, crumpled paper. One of them, a leaf torn from a note-book, contained drawings of faces, intermixed with pictures of all kinds of food. I could recognize at once Mr. and Mrs. Yamada's faces, surrounded with pictures of homely dishes like New Year rice-cakes, red-bean dumplings, sugared chestnuts and fried shrimps, each bearing a caption in endeared language. There were some other faces, one the sweet, serious-looking oval face of a young girl. I thought I had seen that oval face in Mrs. Yamada's house before.

Another sheet bore some pencil writing, hardly legible, because of the weak, trembling hand that had written it, and also because of the lapse of time. After hard deciphering at many places, I understood it to say: "Dear Father and Mother: I am so weak I cannot stand and walk any more. But I am well taken care of by my comrades. I dream of home all the time. We are hiding in woods. Probably I shall die here with many of my comrades, either by the enemy's bombs or of malnutrition. But I do not hate these American boys. I did not hate them from the beginning. I am at peace. So please do not grieve for me." The note, by my best deciphering, was dated in September 1945, the exact day being totally illegible.

The third sheet was a letter from an ex-soldier now living in western Japan, who had been entrusted with these precious pieces of paper by a dying fellow-prisoner at a prisoner's camp in the Philippines. Evidently this dying man had followed Lieutenant Yamada and witnessed his death before he surrendered himself as prisoner. The author of the letter, still a serious malarial patient, had been unable for nearly a year after his return home to locate Lt. Yamada's parents and sincerely regretted the long delay in fulfilling his important mission.

"I am rather glad for the delay," said Mrs. Yamada's brother. "It prolonged my brother-in-law's as well as my sister's life so much longer." I quite agreed with him. At the same time I was grateful for the preservation and final delivery of these rare little documents. There must have been many such messages scribbled on paper or orally given by soldiers on the front, which must have been scattered and wasted as ruthlessly as the lives of their authors themselves.

"My sister felt exactly the same way," said my host. At first Mrs. Yamada wanted to have all the letters, diaries and drawings of her dear boy put in her coffin together with some of her husband's pictures, but later she saw the selfishness of such act. So she willed that they should be all preserved, that some of them be put in print together with similar letters from other dead soldiers, and be read by the war-worn public, and that anything she left, including her husband's paintings, might be used for raising funds for such a project.

Many parents and teachers felt as Mrs. Yamada did about the irreparable sacrifices of their sons and pupils. In the postwar surge toward humanness, their desires and efforts have gradually been organized and materialized, and the long-suppressed voices of the thinking soldiers of the last war have been given a sympathetic hearing by the public. In addition to countless smaller publications, recently two sizable volumes have been published, containing letters and diaries of Japanese student-soldiers who fell in World War II. Hiroshi Yamada's drawings and some of his letters appear in one of them. I was deeply touched in these volumes to find so many young Japanese men asking "What is war? and Why do we kill the enemy we do not hate?" Not only these soldiers but many hundreds of thousands of young Japanese men on the battlefront must have raised the same question. Only they either did not put their thoughts in writing, or their precious records have been lost.

I well remember the dark, puzzled faces my boy-cousins and my husband's students invariably wore when they left for the front. The high-sounding ideals our militarists had fashioned around the Emperor-worship and "the East Asia Co-prosperity Sphere" did not foul them. They hated war, and could not hate the Allied soldiers. But they could not answer the question themselves, and while in this doubting state, they simply did as they were told. What greater tragedy was there than this?

I believe that not only Japanese boys but also boys of many other countries were haunted by the same doubt while fighting. And as far as I know personally, very few of these doubting soldiers came home even when the terrible war had ended. They perished on the battlefield with their question unanswered. It is the duty of humanity to answer it.

21. Groping

The Yamada's war-worn house passed into the possession of Mrs. Yamada's brother. He took in several of his own and his wife's relatives, most of whom were ex-evacuées returning to the city, or repatriates from Manchuria.

I wondered what Ayako would do now. She was a shy girl and did not talk much to me. But she said that she had no intention of going back to her sister's home, nor did she wish to live with her former housemaid. She added that Ohisa had just married the recently repatriated son of ex-Baron Shiba, Ayako's maternal cousin, for whom Ohisa's brother had built the house next door to his. I thought I could understand Ayako's disinclination to be mixed up with these people. Suddenly she disappeared, after hastily saying good-by to my family one day while I was away. I was worried but was too occupied just then with the affairs of my own family. Gradually she slipped from my mind.

Nearly a year later Mrs. Suzuki's older boy unexpectedly called at our house, saying that he had been visiting his old neighbors. We were overjoyed to see him safely back from China and flung question after question at him. We had heard nothing about Baron O's wonderful chauffeur, his wife and little boy since our old neighborhood had been burnt down and they had moved away to the suburbs of Yokohama. But the veteran's face turned dark when I mentioned his mother. My good old neighbor had died. She was caught in the burning of Yokohama.

"I did not know it for more than a year," the boy said thoughtfully. "But even if I had returned home at once after the surrender, I would not have seen her." Then he told us the story of his postwar wanderings.

He belonged, during the latter part of the war, to a transport regiment in the China Expeditionary Army of the Japanese Armed Forces. He was stranded in the vast plains of central China at the time of Japan's surrender. Evidently low-grade officers like him were free, after the regiment was disbanded on the spot, to do whatever they chose. He had no thought of hurrying home, because according to Japanese tradition, a soldier must come home victorious. If not victorious, where could he go?

The Chinese Nationalist army invited the disbanded Japanese soldiers to join them, and promised good pay and charming women. But Corporal Suzuki and another soldier-refugee decided to go over to the other side of the Nationalist-Communist fight for power that had come up to the surface the moment the Japanese military hold had collapsed.

"Why did you decide to go over to the other side?" I asked, being very curious.

These two Japanese soldiers had previously had an edifying experience, so Yukio Suzuki explained, with Chinese Communists. During their war with the Chinese, some men of their regiment were taken prisoners by the Hsin-ssu Army. On receiving repeated messages from the enemy commander that he was willing to release the prisoners unconditionally if some one was sent for them from the Japanese camp, the regimental commander, after much suspicious hesitation, finally sent a delegation, in which Corporal Suzuki was included. The young Japanese officers were impressed by the well-mannered, well-fed, well-disciplined Red soldiers. Moreover, they found there a considerable number of Japanese and Korean men holding active offices. These men told them what they were doing in the Red army.

They compared this Chinese army with their own regiment, where the upper echelons monopolized the use of the motor-trucks and the precious gasoline for requisitioning and carrying away things from Chinese farmers, all for boisterous banquets of their own. On the other hand, the common soldiers, hungry and tired out on their hopeless, endless foot marches over the illimitable surface of the Chinese Continent, often grew insane out of sheer exhaustion and despair, and dropped out of the marching column, never to return. Corporal Suzuki and his men used to go out and pick up the bodies of these boys. There they lay, so far away from home, in woods and marshlands of the southern Yangtee valley, often in groups of twos and threes embracing each other tightly in mutual sword thrusts!

Then the surrender came. Red China enticed some young men of the dissipated Japanese army westward to the heart of Asia, instead of returning to their native islands in the eastern ocean.

The corporal and his companion, unable to tell where the communist territory began, and hoping to get access to the Palu Army, first went to Peking. They wandered in and out of the intricate lanes of the poor quarters of the city, where many desperate ex-soldiers of Japan nested. Whenever they came across a likely Chinese, they whispered to him that they had some firearms to sell. Traffic in firearms was going on openly with the Nationalists, but any deal of this nature with Communists had to be carried on in top secrecy at that time.

One day they met an old man who showed a keen interest in Brownings and Colts. They followed him to his shop and as soon as the door was closed behind them, Yukio Suzuki whispered to him, "Aren't you a communist agent?" Instantly a woman behind him, a tiny, weak old woman, pointed a revolver at the intruder. "Give us permits to get to the Palu

Army," they pleaded. The old man grinned, and the woman brought out *kaoliang* wine. The man then wrote out permits. The woman peeled a panel off the floor, grabbed out two thick pads of paper money and thrust them into the pockets of the astonished Communist applicants.

The only problem left was how to break through the Nationalist parole line. Meanwhile they had come across a few other Japanese ex-soldiers who wanted to get into the communist territory, so they put on Chinese peasants' costume, slipped their permits into the bottom of their shoes, and started westward.

Outside the city gate they bought a bunch of persimmons at a roadside stall. "You Japanese soldiers going to the Palu Army, eh?" the vendor said. "Go straight to the pass."

Now they came to a fork in the road. While they stood wondering, the leader of the party suddenly cried, "Everyone hide!" A Nationalist policeman approached the leader. "You are going to the Palu Army, eh?" he said. "Call your companions from their hiding places. I will show you the way."

Traveling a little distance, the policeman abruptly disappeared, saying that the figure seen in the distance was the police chief, whom he did not wish to meet just then.

"You are going to the Palu Army, eh?" whispered the police chief to the leader. "How many fellows have you got with you? Call them all out of hiding. I will take you all to the pass if you pay me 10,000 yen a person."

The bargain was readily concluded and the party of Japanese refugees were conducted to the boundary pass. They filled the pocket of the Nationalist patrolman and were sent off with a friendly farewell.

Once within the Communist land, they were welcomed everywhere and most courteously relayed on from camp to camp into the hilly paths of Shansi. Sometimes their kind guides carried the unaccustomed travellers on their backs over pools of treacherous muddy water. Some companions decided to stay permanently in the Palu Army, but Yukio and a few others went farther west and finally arrived at the Chinese Communists' general headquarters.

However, they found Yenan already emptied of Japanese refugees. Freedom of association had just been guaranteed to the Japanese people by their new National Constitution, and the political prisoners who had filled the prisons of Japan had been set free, a signal for all overseas political exiles to come home and take part in the building of a free democratic Japan.

The young vagabonds suddenly got homesick and immediately started back. Their journey home seemed far more tedious than their westward march. Arriving finally in their native country, for the first time they realized that their towns, homes, families and possessions had been wiped out long since.

"But you have seen the wide world," I said with a desire to cheer him up.

"Yes, I have," the young man responded warmly. "And I have learned to look to a happy future too." Then he said he was a Communist. I was not surprised, because this newly admitted political theory was quite sensationally popular among the Japanese people at that time, and to say "I am a communist" sounded no different than to say "I am a Christian," "a socialist," "a royalist," etc. etc.

Then he said that he was married and living then with his wife's family because of the housing difficulty. His parents-in-law did not mind his being a Communist, but they did definitely object to his sleeping late in the morning. As a matter of fact, his mother-in-law was the absolute ruler of the household. She made everyone in the family, from her husband—a dignified Chinese-style bone-setter—to her daughters and son-in-law, get up exactly at six o'clock every morning, sun or rain, and take part in the kitchen work and the cleaning of the house and garden, which had to be immaculate and shining each day.

"That's quite democratic," I commented. "Men and women, old and young, all standing on the same ground."

"But terribly mechanical," the young Communist protested.

"What happens if you don't get up at six o'clock in the morning?" I asked.

"The mother says that any one wanting to sleep over may go away to wherever he likes and sleep as much as he pleases, but never in her house."

I laughed with amusement, and thought that it was time for young sons-in-law to have a hard time instead of young daughters-in-law. I told him that he might sleep in our house at any time of the day, if he did not mind our crowded rooming condition.

When he was leaving us, he quite casually asked if we knew a young woman by the name of Ayako Kawashima.

"How do you know her?" I exclaimed with delighted surprise.

He had met the girl at a dance party. She was a good dancer and told him that she had once lived in this neighborhood, but that was all. He did not know exactly where she lived or what she was doing.

Yukio Suzuki never appeared again in spite of my invitation to use our house whenever he needed extra sleep. I lost track of him; and with him, Ayako, momentarily touched with a rosy halo, vanished too.

22. A Free Marriage

One Sunday afternoon when I was looking for the house of a friend of mine in the hopelessly crooked lanes which still abound in the remaining residential parts of Tokyo, some one called my name, and there stood Ayako smiling before me. She looked extremely pretty, although just as shabbily dressed as ever. She said she lived in that neighborhood and asked me to come over to her house if I had time to spare.

Her "home" consisted of a single tiny room in a tumbling-down house in a dingy corner of the lane. She told me that she was working in a nursery home and that she had just been married. "Congratulations!" I cried in sincere joy. Explaining her husband's absence, she said that he had to work in his factory on Sundays, too. He was mending scrap cars and was fright-

fully busy. "Why, you an ex-peeress marrying a factory hand!"
I almost cried aloud, but just controlled myself.

"You don't mind my telling you that he is a Communist?"
she said, taking me completely aback.

"Why did you marry a Communist?" I asked after recovering myself.

"Because I am a Communist myself," Ayako answered with
a self-confident smile. "I knew him slightly before he was called
to service. Communism drew us together when the terrible war
was over and we both found ourselves forlorn survivors."

Takashi was the son of the gardener formerly in service in
Ayako's parental household. He was recuited to the army just
before the Pacific War broke out, and sent to Indo-China. She
saw him at a distance then, but had since been too occupied
with other things to remember him. Six and a half years later,
at a communists' gathering, she was introduced to a young
man, in whose square, robust figure she at once recognized the
shy, uniformed boy whom his humble-mannered father had
brought to say good-by to her. What a sweeping change had
since come on the country and the people!

Their sympathy for each other's war-bereavement developed
into love. "I was terrified at first," Ayako confided to me, "to
realize that I was entirely free to love and marry any one in the
world." Takashi felt the same way. So they celebrated their
wedding all by themselves, under a wild paulownia tree, she
whispered to me, whose flaming flowers burnt intoxicating incense before the altar of the starry heaven. "This is true marriage," she said. "My first one was only a series of dead cere-

monies." I had never seen her so eloquent, passionate and straightforward.

"How did you ever happen to become a Communist?" I could not help asking her.

Ayako then told me the story of how she left the Yamada house and was picked up by Communists. After the passing on of Mrs. Yamada she had found herself extremely uncomfortable among the new inmates who had come to fill the house. She thought of a cousin of hers who had evacuated into the country with his family during the war but who, she hoped, had returned to Tokyo by that time and would now give her some help or advice. However she found his city house occupied by strangers. The mistress of the house haughtily eyed Ayako and said that she did not know where the former owner lived.

The place was not far from the site of her former parents-in-law's mansion. She knew they had gone to live with their married daughter, so she walked up toward the familiar neighborhood. It was still completely deserted, none of her former neighbors having come back to rebuild on the old sites. Alone, unnoticed, and feeling relieved to meet none of her former acquaintances who would have pitied the changed appearance of the once lovely Lady Ayako, she wandered through the ruins of her former home. The debris of the stone foundations and mud-and-tile walls were still there, untouched and covered with weeds. The iris pond in the centre of the garden was now a small pool of stagnant water. The stream which had once rippled throughout the grounds in graceful curves, was clogged up with dirt and grass. Some of the charred garden trees had been cut down, but some still stood, looking like weather-beaten carcasses of giants.

All the garden flowers, except the *hagi*, had been destroyed, roots and all. The spacious old garden used to have many secluded corners, filled at this time of the year with tall ferns, purple campanulas, sapphire-blue morning glories and Japanese goldenrod. Whenever she had felt irritated or tired with perpetually waiting on her august parents-in-law, she used to slip away into one of these garden nooks to weep and be consoled in the company of the lovely wild flowers.

But flowers had nearly completely disappeared not only from ex-Viscount T's. garden but from nearly all other Japanese gardens. Even the morning glory, once so omnipresent in our Japanese summer, had been practically annihilated. Only the deep-rooted perennial *hagi* had survived and grown fat with the burning. Their long, slender sprays arched up higher than Ayako's head and formed lovely arbors here and there throughout the ruined grounds. Through their feathery leaves the morning sun shone in a thousand shades of soft green and the bunches of their tiny butterfly-shaped flowers were just turning magenta-purple.

Ayako sat down under one of the giant *hagi* bushes and pondered over what she should do now. She tried to think of someone whom she could turn to. All she could think of were women like her sister, mad in pursuit of American luxuries and gaieties, or like many of her schoolmates, worn and desperate in their struggles to keep their impoverished families alive and going. She could remember a few cases of suicide among her close acquaintances. Life seemed totally bereft of meaning.

A breeze suddenly rippled through the bushes of *hagi* flowers and their slender, arched sprays, swaying and rolling, shook off the remnants of morning dew. A few drops, sparkling in the green-dappled sunshine, struck Ayako's face and awakened her from her pensive reverie. How exquisitely old Japanese poets compared the helplessness of human life to a dewdrop on a tremulous *hagi* spray! Were human beings after all helplessly awaiting a wind of fate to brush them off into nothingness?

Hardly had the rustle of the wind stopped when most unexpectedly in the ruined, deserted garden, Ayako heard footsteps. A brightly dressed young woman appeared. Ayako was startled because the woman's face appeared very familiar to her.

"Why! Aren't you Ayako-san?" The woman's voice startled her again and gladdened her heart because she was grateful to be so familiarly called in this place of desolation. But it took her a few moments to recognize in this beautifully painted, sadly smiling woman the highly tanned, care-free, sports-loving girl she used to see at high school.

"So you are alone, too," her old classmate said compassionately, but in a composed voice. From her fresh toilet and a bamboo basket with a wet towel and a vanity case held in her red-nailed hand, Ayako could tell that her friend had been to a bath-house and was on her way home by the short cut through this disowned garden. Most gratefully she accepted the invitation to walk home with her companion.

"Life is joyless, and desolate, isn't it?" Omiyo-san said, sitting in her attractively furnished apartment and smoking a fragrant American cigarette. "You have guessed by now, haven't you, what I am doing?"

It was only five and a half years before that they were graduated from high school. They were all in navy-blue uniforms with white ties, black stockings and black shoes, their short straight hair braided in two bushy pigtails. They sang the national anthem and some of the patriotic songs before the national flag and the pictures of the Emperor and the Empress. The diploma they were given was of thinner paper and smaller size than those earlier graduates had received, but the school principal spoke on the ultimate Japanese victory, the eternal prosperity of the Imperial Family, and the glory of the nation under the divine rule. The girls had believed in all this, though very vaguely.

"I hate to think of those days," Omiyo-san observed. "I hate to meet my old schoolmates, but when I saw you I didn't have that feeling. You seemed to need consoling, even if by a woman like me."

Omiyo-san went on with her story. Her husband was in one of the transport vessels bombed and sunk in the China Sea. At the time of the air-raid of March 10, 1945, she was living with her own family, but while fighting the flames she lost track of them all, and had seen none of them since. Alone, hungry and having nowhere to go, she joined the hosts of street girls who nested in the dark holes they found in the war-debris of the city-deserts.

"You have a handsome apartment, which shows your high

position," Ayako observed, sincerely admiring her friend's dark-grained chest of drawers, red-lacquered mirror-stand, tea-cabinet, electric cooker on a low hardwood table, and lovely colored pillows and bedding—things that belonged to days of long ago.

Omiyo-san candidly confided to her that she had worked up to that position only recently. The last two years she had worked out-of-doors entirely, depending only on the tastes and financial appliance of each of her companions. In rainy weather she went out of business, and had to lie for days in a corner of a leaky, bad-smelling boarding house, drinking water and eating nothing. In winter she went to hot spring resorts, and worked among hotels there. She was most miserable, but novices in this profession had to work up from these levels.

She literally slaved and saved, and finally established herself in a little apartment. "I am grateful to have just a little of settled life now," she remarked. "Through my experience I have thoroughly realized that the only way for a woman to settle down even just a little in this war-wrecked country is the way I am living now."

Ayako thought that there was a great deal of truth in Omiyo-san's observation. She herself was a homeless, penniless and jobless war-widow, not very different from a beggar in the street. She almost felt she would do anything to have a room of her own, livably furnished, where she could be sheltered from the hungry, restless, sad gaze of her fellow creatures. Her marriage to a man whom she did not love had been a kind of prostitution, she thought defiantly. Physical service to a man for money would not be any worse, if not better, than being a slave wife.

"Do you find all men worth your service?" Ayako asked with a warm interest.

"A wife serves, but it's business with me," the proud friend remonstrated. She said that she had to drive each bargain as hard as she could but that most men were just as tight bargainers. They made use of every minute of the contract, like a cat tossing and licking a helpless mouse. "No, I get a thrill out of it," she explained, "because I use art and technique while keeping a cold eye on the man, and come out the winner in the game."

"Don't you sometimes come to feel a sort of attachment to some of the men you meet?"

"No, I don't want to," the proud, despairing heart cried. "That's why I never take the same man twice. I refuse to love any one—anything!"

To Ayako's question whether she took in foreigners sometimes, Omiyo-san nodded yes. Tokyo was full of moneyed foreigners. But Japanese or foreign, men were all alike—hungry animals—the color of their skin, hair or eyes making no difference whatsoever. However, Japanese men with big bundles of money were becoming fewer and fewer. The millionaire country bumpkins, once the best bidders in the street, were rapidly disappearing, so that from now on girls would have to shop chiefly among foreigners.

As for GI's, Omiyo-san said with a twitch around her mouth, they came out into the street in great numbers on their pay-days, and stuffed the girls' pockets with military money. Immediately then came forth the dollar-brokers, who collected the PX money from the pun-pun girls, giving them Japanese money in return at the lowest possible exchange rate, and sold the bills to smugglers of American goods. Thus thrived the traffic across the "off limits" line.

She then added that recently the neighborhood where she was living had been one of the GI's favorite resorts. Very probably the shadowy, secluded ruins of big gardens scattered around there had been the attraction for them, particularly during hot summer nights.

"I hope you won't be shocked," she said, "if I tell you that in the garden of your former parents-in-law's mansion, where you once lived as a chaste and pious daughter-in-law, you now see discarded paper and fish-skin things blown by the wind!"

The world had changed, Omiyo-san argued, for in order to live like a proper human being, there was absolutely no way for a war-outcast woman like herself and Ayako but the way she was living. If Ayako wished, she would gladly introduce her to the staff members of her professional association. Or, if she was too shy for that yet, Ayako, with her past bourgeois-aristocratic upbringing could apply to a certain commission house Omiyo-san knew of. It was situated just outside the city of Tokyo and it handled, under absolute secrecy, applications from ladies of the upper circles and from high-class Occupation men. It was very well paid—a single engagement would enable a pressed ex-countess to feed her incompetent husband, pale-faced children and wailing mother-in-law and herself quite nourishingly for a week, although it would probably not amount to more than thirty dollars of an Occupation gentleman's pocket money. But one needed good clothes and soft hands to be successful along that particular line. Ayako had lost every bit of her costly wardrobe, and her hands had been mercilessly hardened.

The two women sat moodily while the coffee began to boil. The strong aroma of this costly foreign beverage—100 yen a cup!—mingling with the smell of foreign cigarettes, tantalized Ayako with heart-rending nostalgia for her past days of security and comfort. She pondered on what she should do.

Just then some one called outside the sliding door, and a young woman stepped in. She was a type quite opposed to Omiyo-san, but apparently was on friendly terms with her. Omiyo-san introduced her to Ayako as her cousin and a "hot communist."

23. A Free Divorce

Omiyo-san's cousin drew Ayako into the communist world, which evidently seemed entirely wonderful to the displaced ex-peeress who had seen so much selfish abandonment and purposeless patience around her. Unlike the despairing men and women among her old acquaintances, her new friends seemed to be filled to the brim with radiant hopes for the future of mankind, and vigorous enthusiasm. Life suddenly brightened up for her.

Masako not only took in the forlorn war-widow to room with her but also found her a job. This secretary in the mine workers' national league knew many union men who practically controlled the placement of workers. She found the inexperienced Ayako a position as a nursery teacher. Ayako's volunteer service for the care of children during the war was favorably taken into consideration for that purpose.

Ayako, who had never thought she could get a job of this kind, was completely fascinated by the work, which assured her a purpose in life and economic independence. Even after her marriage she went on with it with unchanged enthusiasm.

I think it was in the early spring of 1949 that Ayako came to see me. She asked me to act as interpreter for the negotiations which were going on concerning the nursery home where she worked. This nursery took care of the children of the mothers working in a big factory now under the supervision of the Occupation Army. But it also took in some children of the neighborhood. It was allowed the use of an old wooden building and the open ground around it, located in the outer compound of the factory establishment. There, some sixty-five children and babies were tended by Ayako and two other nurses. The nursery was financed by the labor union which sent workers to the factory. It collected some fees from the parents and received frequent distributions of Lara gifts, so it was quite well-off, and Ayako and her colleagues had been working there very happily.

Quite recently, however, some of the mothers suddenly declared that they were going to withdraw their children and send them to a new nursery school which a new labor union formed by some workers of the same factory, had just opened. The new nursery had already taken away more than half of the children of the old one.

The root of the matter was that the old labor union was dominated by Communists, which the factory management found no longer tolerable. Consequently they let it be known they would welcome a new union, free from all communist tinge, and formed exclusively by the workers of the same factory. The new nursery was a by-product of this shifting plan of the management.

The nursery teachers, including Ayako, resented this interference and were also afraid of losing their jobs. The leaders of the old union were furious. They went to see the Japanese manager of the factory workers first, but finding him uncooperative, went to the Occupation officer in charge of the factory's labor questions.

Ayako was not at all sure what the American officer, with his flushed face and an excited manner, said. She, as well as the rest of the group, could only follow the interpreter, a swaggering, unlovely Japanese man, according to Ayako's comment, who in a very commanding way said that the old union, communist-dominated and subversive, should be at once dissolved. All the workers in the factory must join the new union. The old nursery was of course to be immediately closed. Then he harangued about the vices of the Communists, calling them the enemy of the benevolent Occupation rule and traitors to the Japanese nation, who deserved to be bundled together and machine-gunned.

He simply sneered at the protest Ayako's group tried to make, and flatly refused to translate it to the Occupation officer. They wanted to say that, in the beginning days of the Occupation when the Allied supervision encouraged labor unions to be formed in all fields of employment throughout the country, Communists were the first to rally to the project. They practically started the labor unions of postwar Japan. In the particular case of this nursery, the communist union leaders themselves got together the women of this particularly war-devastated neighborhood, found them employment in the factory, and with the encouraging support of the factory management, organized the nursery for their benefit. And now, without a single word of consultation or even of gratitude, they were to be discarded in favor of a handful of subservient men fawning on authority. Could this be called democratic? The interpreter thrust them out of the office and shut the door on them.

They now wanted to see the same Occupation officer once more and talk with him through an interpreter who would more faithfully convey their points of view. So Ayako was there, she said, to ask that I help them.

I was busy at that time working for Admiral Toyoda's trial, but felt I should go. I thought it was a pity that some Occupation officers and the Japanese people under their supervision were being made distrustful of each other simply because of the interpreters. Due to the practical incommensurability of the English and Japanese languages, the Occupation had to depend a great deal on the degree of intelligence and moral integrity of the "go-betweens." I had previously come across several cases where the interpreter was apparently more anxious to please the master than to convey truthfully differing thoughts and views.

Obtaining special permission to cut my office hours at the

War Crimes Court, I went with Ayako's group to meet the American officer. I found him perfectly amiable and fair-minded, and willing to discuss the matter squarely on an equal footing with the Japanese complainants. I did my best to present truthfully the views of both sides and bring about an amicable understanding.

The gentle-faced, quiet-voiced lieutenant colonel said that the Allied supervision did not interfere with the affairs of the workers in either forming a union, or running a nursery so long as these did not affect the efficiency of the factory work. But since the present existence of two unions and two nurseries was causing disputes among the workers and lessening their efficiency, the Allied supervision had decided that there should be a single union and a single nursery; that because of frequent cases of theft occurring within the factory, all outsiders were requested to stay away from the compound as much as possible, and consequently were requested not to take part in the union activities to be conducted by the workers of the factory. As for the nurseries, the mothers were to decide which of the two they should keep for their children.

Ayako's negotiating party was dissatisfied because they realized that eventually their old union would be thrown out of that big factory, and the nursery question handed over to the mothers who, unable to finance the undertaking by themselves, would sooner or later put it under the control of the bosses of the new union. Decidedly it was the defeat of the old union.

Being a complete stranger, I could not clearly see the complication of the general situation. Moreover, I felt extremely confused when I tried to interpret for the secretary of the old union who headed the negotiating party. Evidently he was deep in the Communists' tenets on "Tactics" and was carefully maneuvering on that foothold, but I could not quickly respond to his frame of mind. As far as the nursery issue was concerned, I thought the colonel was fair and very democratic to say that the mothers had the right of decision. It left room for Ayako and others connected with the nursery still to work in. I thought the meeting quite successful, and when we came out of the colonel's office, I gave an exact account of the conference to the mothers who had been anxiously awaiting outside to know the result. Technically speaking, I was simply an interpreter and had no right to speak to the mothers, but they asked me questions and my habit of plain speaking just came out.

Suddenly I noticed the displeasure of the union people at my free talks with the mothers. Evidently they wanted to keep them under control and I was unintentionally counteracting their plan. Ayako appeared extremely embarrassed, so I took hasty leave of them and came home.

Several weeks later I got a letter from Ayako, reporting that by the mothers' decision the two nurseries had been united into one and that Ayako, by their request, continued to hold the position of a teacher there, although her communist associates, who had lost hold of the issue, called her a deserter. She said that she was so attached personally to the work that she could not leave it then, even if her communist friends repudiated her. The nursery, with mothers and children and all, she commented, was primarily a beachhead for the Communists' tactical advance, where welfare or misery of individuals was to be subordinated to the importance of their strategic plans.

She added that she had once suggested that the nursery work would be more effectively carried on if it was conducted side by side with birth-control guidance, because some mothers, through their ignorance and lack of forethought, had babies in close succession and rapidly burdened the nursery as well as themselves. She, like many other thoughtful Japanese people, claimed that in the over-populated and war-impoverished Japan, birth-control was one of the most basic remedies for the cruel family tragedies of mentally and materially bankrupt parents killing their children and themselves—tragedies occurring daily in countless numbers. But her comrades laughed at her ignorance of communist theories and told her that such ideas only profited the enemy.

Some time later she surprised me by writing that she had got a divorce from her husband. She said she could no longer stand Takashi's ever-hardening view that the world was divided into two opposing camps and that every human being had to stand on this side or the other of the dividing line. In the early days of its restoration under the Occupation, communism in Japan seemed to stand for the happiness of the people, but now it emphasized the hatred of its enemy more than anything else, whatever this "enemy" was. Hatred, particularly when it was over-emphasized, was most distasteful to Ayako's Buddhist heart, which consequently could no longer follow her husband's party activities. The decisive issue was her insistence on working for the nursery even after its disconnection with communist influence. This Takashi denounced as an act benefiting the enemy.

"It was a totally new discovery," Ayako wrote, "when I fell in love with Takashi. 'A woman is free to love a man,' I repeated a thousand times within myself. But now I have discovered another freedom. A woman is also free to reject a man!"

I thoroughly understood what Ayako meant by her discovery of two freedoms. Japanese women under the feudal rule had long been denied the right to choose a husband. Falling in love with a man was a social crime for them and divorce—from the wife's point of view—was too often worse than death. The sweeping changes, accompanying the war have given many of them these freedoms now, but only in rugged, thorny forms. It will require time, patient efforts and steady wisdom for women to refine and secure these precious rights to the democratic advantage of the Japanese people.

In Ayako's case, I felt sad that her two discoveries had come in such close succession.

24. Hard Road

The last time I saw Ayako was more than a year ago. She spoke about her work with enthusiasm, saying that she and two other girls were closely cooperating with the mothers to maintain their rights in the management of the nursery, which occasionally suffered unfair, undemocratic interferences from the bosses of the new labor union to which the mothers now belonged. In cooperation with some other nurseries they had started study groups for social problems, including birth-control. Lack of funds she said, was the gravest drawback. She lived then with Masako, her original Communist friend, who evidently understood her point of view, although most of her former coworkers had repudiated her.

I felt in her a bubbling zest for life and a poise of the mind which both come from confidence and satisfaction in one's work. She had grown remarkably.

Ayako's case has drawn my special interest because she is typical of Japanese women who have been suddenly liberated from the fetters of the old social and family customs but who, through deprivations and trials of their new environment, have sincerely searched for the true meaning of liberation. Ayako was brought up under the strong influence of her Buddhist grandmother. She could not, even through the overwhelming changes of her circumstances, get away from the idea of Buddha's charity and human kindness. She has steadily worked up to where she is now. She is the kind of girl who cannot feel happy unless others are happy too. What she demands is the freedom to measure the width of human kindness. I now hope that she will find a man who fits into her frame of mind and heart and will heal the vacancy she has suffered from the dissolution of her short second marriage. Although a woman is free to reject a man, a happy marriage is far more fruitful for a free woman. What counts is not the freedoms in themselves, but the fruits of these noble human rights.

I have known many other cases of liberated Japanese women

struggling for the right use and development of their new environment. Every one of them now knows that economic independence is the crucial step for any social freedom of sound and fruitful nature. And no doubt, the possibility of women's economic independence has been greatly enlarged by our postwar economic and legislative changes. In other words, the first clearing has been made on which Japanese women must by themselves build their highway for democracy.

As a woman I tend to measure the present democratic growth of our people primarily by our women's social gains. I am definitely pleased with some of the things I see around me today. At the same time, however, I cannot overlook the sobering fact that vast responsibilities and burdens now weigh heavily on us women of Japan. Our failure to carry them out with stern, resolute efforts will mean the destruction of our national life and utter misery to our children.

The fact that we should not be too optimistic has been thoroughly shown recently through my personal involvement in two divorce cases within my family circle. In both of them I have fought and am still fighting hard on the wife's side against the tenacious clinging of man to his feudal privileges. These two husbands, while applauding the democratic principles whenever these were beneficial to their own personal interests, stuck tightly to the old tradition of a husband withholding his wife's possessions in case the divorce came through the wife's choice or through her fault. In either case the wife was turned out with only her clothes, her money and some other possessions being confiscated by the husband. This custom originated in our feudal family system where the husband was the master and the wife his slave, whose possessions were consequently to be totally surrendered to his control. In case of divorce, only when the issue rose entirely through the fault of the husband's family did the wife get back all of her dowry. Any money brought by the wife was generally considered as a gift from the wife's family to the husband's, and consequently withheld by the husband's family when the wife was divorced for whatever reason.

In both our family cases, the husband made up excuses so that the divorce might appear due to the wife's wilfulness. Thus he might withhold a part of her belongings. One husband turned over the only child entirely to the wife's responsibility and refused to give a cent toward its support. The other husband said that the wife might take either of the two children but that she was not to expect any material assistance from him for the child's maintenance and education. The wife thought she could not keep either of her children under such conditions.

I thought it was unbelievable that such husbands should and could exist in our present democratic Japan. So I tried hard to persuade them to be reasonable and manly enough to respect their wives' basic human rights. But I failed, and had to realize that it was a fight against a tradition of centuries and not against individual men. I knew that the newly democratized law was there, ready to protect the wife, but it required money, time and tedious procedure to have that law work effectively. In either case, the wife had no money to start a suit.

The fact is that the present democracy in Japan has been

framed and grafted onto Japanese soil by external agencies. It has been given a complete legislative framework on which it is expected to grow and ripen into a fully functioning organism. It must be remembered, however, that the Japanese soil has never been productive for the people's democratic growth. The feudal society of the people, kept intact through the many centuries of our isolation, owed its security and remarkably long life entirely to its adherence to the principle of the total suppression of basic human rights—that is, absolute obedience to authority and sacrifice of the individual to the glory of the whole. That old Japan, some may argue, was opened to the world nearly a century ago and the country has since been modernized at great speed. These changes, however, have been mainly superficial, while the basic social relations and sentiments of the people have remained practically unchanged. The recent war and the drastic reforms carried out by the Occupation have no doubt reached far deeper into our national life than any of the previous changes. It is earnestly hoped that the present democratization efforts will really break through the hard core of the long outdated social sentiments of the people, and set up the nation on a thorough and sound modern basis. Through experience we have learned that modern influences on a people who have not outgrown their feudal outlook, often work dangerous and wasteful consequences.

The road to the democratization of Japan is still pretty rough. As for divorce, we may say that our women have become able to get it through their own initiative much more easily and that such divorces do occur quite frequently now, but that the majority of these cases provide the wife with practically nothing in the way of material resources. The general public sentiment toward this question at present is that a wife is free to leave her husband, and also free to take the children with her, provided she is able to support herself and the children. And our present economic conditions often drive and also enable women to accept these hard terms.

Although I was greatly disappointed in the results of the two divorce cases in my own family, I must add that I did have a cheerful experience in one of them. In this case, the wife appealed to the family court of the little provincial town in western Japan where her husband lived.

Our present law says that a divorce may be effected simply through mutual agreement of the parties concerned and requires no court procedure. If the parties cannot agree, either side may call upon the arbitration of the family court and if the case is still unsettled, litigation may be sought. Divorce by mutual agreement is apt to be abused by a selfish husband or parent-controlled son who, through this institution, is able to divorce his wife by simply forcing her to sign the divorce instrument or forging her signature on it and showing it at the registration office. Consequently, more women than men today are finding cause to appeal for public arbitration. At any rate, a divorce case, before it is brought to law, must always be considered by the family court, located, so the law prescribes, nearest to the husband's actual place of residence.

The wife in my case had lived in Tokyo since her forced separation. In order to obtain the aid of the family court, she had to make several expensive trips at her own expense, to the little provincial town in western Japan where her husband lived. I accompanied her once. I found the two country gentlemen who made up the board, as well as the presiding judge, very sympathetic to the wife. After hard persuasion they finally succeeded in having the husband give the wife 300,000 yen as compensation for the enormous sum of money, totalling tens of millions of yen in the present inflated currency, expended by the wife and her parents to help the husband to qualify as a practicing physician. The compensation may appear miserably small in proportion to the great contributions made by the wife and her family toward the welfare of the husband. The husband originally claimed that he would be generous enough to return to the wife all the things she had brought with her at the time of marriage, but that he had no obligation whatsoever to hand over to her any of the things she had acquired for him after marriage. This claim was quite in accordance with the traditional feudal custom. Any effort on the part of the arbitration board to get the wife compensated was a gain for her. Our present law declares that all possessions acquired after marriage are common property of the husband and wife, of which the wife, in case of divorce, has the right to claim a third. But in present Japan, as I have explained, law is one thing and common practice is another.

The arbitration board listened attentively to the wife's claims as well as to my testimony and explanations. Then they said that, unlike big progressive cities like Toyko, in their conservative little country town there was no precedent of this kind.

What they were doing was the furthest they could go against the husband's terrible conservatism. I saw a sincerely cooperative attitude in them. I was also happy to find, in this country court where the arbitration board sat, various posters hung on the walls, encouraging and urging women's participation in the defense and administration of the "people's law." I could not fail to see the buds of democracy sprouting through the cracks of feudal conservatism.

Perhaps I have discussed the present democratic tendencies in Japan too much from the women's point of view, but that angle is most personal to me. There are, however, other happy auguries. Our children have been given more serious consideration as a social group. Young people have come to have a louder voice in the general affairs of the people. A constitutional government has been restored. The clerks in government offices have discarded their authoritative manners of the old days, becoming friendly toward the people and a little more efficient in the carrying of their business. Above all, freedom of thought and speech has been guaranteed, and although there is still some restriction laid on it, our people now enjoy these freedoms to a degree unprecedented in our past. It is so good to think and openly talk of our people as a part of humanity and not as a race divinely chosen to serve the Imperial Descendants of the Great Sun-Goddess! Despite the discouraging facts often pointed out, I, as an admirer of patient, sincere, constructive work—particularly in the present world of sweeping views and tearing schisms—have great hope for the future growth of the Japanese people.

Part Six

THE OCCUPATION AND THE PEACE TREATY

---

25. Summing Up: A Japanese View of the Occupation

The Occupation has run its course. When we look back at its early days and see what fast recovery the country has made, we are filled with gratitude for the help and guidance given this war-shattered nation.

We were literally naked and starved when the Allied forces landed in the Japanese islands. Most of our cities had been reduced to wilderness where the most primitive mode of life was barely kept up. But today, buildings have gone up and are still going up everywhere. City streets are lined with rebuilt shops, loaded with commodities. People in the street are better and more carefully dressed today than during or even before the war. Black-marketeering has practically disappeared, and normal free economy returned to stabilize our daily life to a notable degree.

The traffic throughout the country has been put in reasonable or even comfortable order. The black nights where we burnt tiny and frightfully expensive candles seem to be stories of long ago now that our cities are flooded with neonlights. The housewives who used to cook their meagre food by chopping embers from the ruined houses now have gas to cook by. The children who once played "evacuation" and "we have nothing to eat today," have wonderful toys of all kinds in colorful plastics and nylons. Our gardens, public and private, once given over to plots of potatoes and radishes, are once more gay with our old familiar flowers.

"Why, everything has come back as of the prewar days," we say to each other with a mixture of wonder and gratitude, but hastily add with a bitterness in our hearts, "except the purchasing power of our inflated paper money!" We have to remember that a pretty toy teapot a little girl is playing with by the roadside costs as much in *yen* today as a man could have lived comfortably on for a month in the prewar days. But just the same we sincerely admit that we never expected to see our country recover to this extent in less than seven years.

The Allied Occupation of Japan must have been the most liberal and kindly of military occupations recorded in history. The Japanese people were first puzzled and surprised at its leniency, remembering their own national experiences in military conquests of other peoples. They have since taken full advantage of the goodwill of the victors.

With all its abundant benefits, we must own that the Occupation, as a natural sequence to the terrible Pacific and East Asian Wars, was a hard experience for us. We shall never forget the days when we beheld for the first time the magnificent Occupation setup in the midst of our war devastation. We were a nation of desperate people, hungry, ragged and filth-covered. Our entire national system was shattered to pieces. Planting itself in the midst of the hordes of such people, the Occupation Army had naturally to draw a definite "off limits" line around it for the sake of defending its security and efficiency. That line had to be determined necessarily by a very technical, discriminatory mechanism where nationality was all-important and individuals did not count. And that line was to mark the sharp boundary between abundance and hunger, rainbow-colored cleanliness and gray sordidness, privileged victors and a nation in bondage.

The effects of the luxuries and comforts of American life, brought over *en masse*, naturally instigated crimes among the destitute Japanese people. The sight of even a single cigarette, a spoonful of sugar or a tiny cake of soap, to say nothing of other and more delectable luxuries, pricked and goaded the long-suppressed nerves of the brutalized Japanese. Every one of these was an unattainable prize to them. Transactions of any kind with regard to Allied goods were forbidden between the Allied personnel and the Japanese nationals. Stealing became rampant and other illicit methods followed. Particularly for young people, the temptation was irresistibly powerful, and for some time we felt as if we were turning into a race of thieves, smugglers, black-marketeers, prostitutes and monkeys. Of all the hard experiences of the war, nothing seemed to me more miserable than the frantic rush of some Japanese people around the fringes of the off-limits line in the early Occupation years.

Gradually, however, with increases in food supplies and clothing material, particularly cotton goods, some degree of morale has been restored. It was around the fifth year of the Occupation that food finally became obtainable at least for the minimum subsistence rate. It was only after 1951 that clothing material, silk or cotton, (although no woolens yet) could be bought in small amounts for homes like ours.

This economic recovery of the country was entirely due to the generous American help, and the "special procurement boom" brought to the country by the Korean War. With it, law and order has been restored in our national life. Our police system has been greatly strengthened. Our streets have been cleared of gangsters and prostitutes, at least during daytime, and the strong autonomous organizations of these outlaws have been effectively suppressed. Filth and war-refugees' hovels have been put out of public sight. Petty thefts have markedly lessened, although murders and suicides seem to go on at the same alarming rates. At least our patched washings in our backyard stopped disappearing and the bunch of empty milk bottles at our front door now safely waits for the milkman to take back. It is good to be assured that one's possessions are a little safer today than they used to be, particularly when those possessions are still scanty and therefore that much more valuable.

Criticism has often been made that this restoration of law

and order has been realized at the cost of the democratic growth of the people; that the increase in the number of policemen, newly armed with clubs and pistols in place of the clattering swords of the old days, means not only the effective suppression and prosecution of crimes but also the ruthless nipping in the bud of that free thinking and free action so warmly fostered in the early days of the Occupation. The strengthening of police power means that the ruling class and bureaucracy, after the temporary setback, are fast settling back into their old mold. Some people go so far as to say that in the early days of the Occupation all Japan went to the extreme left and now it has swung back to the extreme right and thus the task of the Occupation ends in total failure; that the Japanese people have come full circle, and look and act as if nothing had happened to them in the past decade!

The freedom of thought, speech and action we enjoyed in the anarchical condition of the country in the early postwar period did seem to promise something different from what we actually have today. It is undeniable that a rule of authority, backed with strong police power, appears to be coming back today. Liberal thinking and a critical approach have come to be often considered "pinkish." But we must not overlook the fact that we still have some room left for our democratic claims, room in which to fight and control the menace of the return of fascism. This is the most essential part of the gain and advance we have accomplished under the rule and guidance of the Occupation.

If anyone has felt any degree of disillusionment in the work of the Occupation, it is because he has expected too much of human history. The primary aim of the Occupation was to reconstruct fascist-devastated, war-crushed Japan into a modern democratic nation. The Occupation authorities, with the victor's magnaminity and high ideals drew up plans for the democratization of Japan. With abundant economic help and well-equipped military protection they saw that these plans were effectively carried out.

The democratization of Japan, however, did not progress as speedily and effectively as was at first hoped. It was hard, no doubt, for the Americans who have opened a great continent and built a civilization on the principles of individual freedom and vast economic resources, to understand the mentality and the essential economic and social problems of the Japanese people. The Japanese lived for countless centuries in their narrow archipelago under stern feudal economy and barbaric methods of birth-control. On coming in contact with modern industrialism, they suddenly bulged out in population and colonial ambition, only, however, to lose in the last war all their territories and shrink back to their original islands. Their enormously swollen population now presented a more serious problem than ever. There seems to be scarcely a single point in common between the vast, continental civilization of America and the singularly insular Japanese culture. This may account for the fact that the democratization plans, drawn by American specialists after sympathetic studies of our circumstances and with sincere well-wishing for our people, have sometimes proved to be too expensive and too unrealistic for this poor island nation to follow.

The language barrier was another great drawback. Not only the incommensurability of the English and the Japanese language but also the plain, direct speaking habit of the Americans, and the slippery ellipticism of the Japanese, all worked toward causing undue impatience and distrust on the part of the Occupation authorities and unnecessary fear and aversion on the part of the Japanese people. Liaison came to assume undue importance. Hosts of interpreters, naturally without too careful selection, were allowed to control the broad technical and mental gap between the two languages. Frequently I heard complaints made by Japanese about the inefficiency or even dishonesty of some of the interpreters and the inability of some Occupation authorities to discern sincerity or insincerity in the Japanese people. Even taking into account the jealousy of the complainants against those in favor of the Occupation authorities, I could not but admit that these complaints were often well grounded.

Another factor that hampered the smooth progress of Japan's democratization program was the most unhappy division of the Allied powers into two antagonistic groups. Japan was lucky to be occupied under the single dominance of the United States and not divided in the middle like Germany and Korea. Still, the tension was acutely felt by the country. The single purpose of the Occupation now came to be doubly affected, and in counteraction to the growing tendency to the extreme left, it was but natural that the extreme rightist forces should regain strength, with intolerance and vindictiveness again coming in between. This was most unfortunate for the Japanese people, who had just started so hopefully on their road for democratic freedom and tolerance. They really needed more time and a little more peaceful environment for attaining basic growth in order to function as a sound constitutional nation.

What perpetually puzzled any naïve mind was the fact that the fostering of democracy in Japan was to be carried out under the hard-set discriminatory mechanism of the Occupation. But the Occupation was a military affair, being a continuation of the state of war. It necessarily rested, despite the democratic traditions of the Allied army, on military law and absolutism. No military organization can be democratic in the civil and constitutional sense. It must be supported by military law which holds the security and integrity of that military organization above individual freedom and basic human rights, and which allows each superior a degree of absolutism and arbitrary personal consideration over his subordinates. Unless we understood thoroughly and accepted this peculiar situation as the only possible one under the circumstances, we were apt to get the impression that the democratization of Japan under the Occupation was primarily a matter of form.

In the offices of the Occupation, people of various nationalities worked and were paid on a nationality basis, and had different privileges. Some of the nationality regulations maintained in these offices were hard to face, such as having one's possessions examined each time one went out of the office building, and being allowed to use only designated quarters.

The Japanese employees in the Occupation were paid by the

Japanese government and I got one of the highest salaries on the scale. I once had it whispered to me that our monthly salary was practically equal to a day's pay for those who did about the same kind and amount of work with us, but on the American payroll. When we consider the difference in the purchasing power of the American dollars and Japanese yen, and other actual circumstances, this comparison did not seem too much of an exaggeration.

It is true that many Japanese workers in the Occupation offices had a very poor command of English and therefore deserved lower payment, since the Occupation business had to be carried out primarily in English. But I knew some young girls, born in America but brought up and educated in Japan in just about the same way as most middle-class Japanese girls had been, who enjoyed all the privileges of the Allied personnel in the Occupation, while some women, born in Japan and educated in America, worked on the other side of the "off limits" line. The American people who worked with us—many of them young *nisei* boys—knew this hard fact about the payment discrimination and were very considerate about it. So most of the time we put it out of our minds, but it sometimes led to the indulgence of the Allied supervisers and the wilful laziness of the Japanese workers, and thus to the deterioration of the Occupation business.

"Just remember," said some people, "that the entire nation are prisoners of war, and be grateful for the freedom allowed us." "Remember," said others, "what the Japanese army did in their occupied territories." Strangely, when such remarks were made by Japanese people I always found myself giving ready and hearty approval, while any similar allusions made by any of the Occupation people hurt me bitterly, because I did not want them to make any comparison between the fallen Japanese military and the American army in which I had hope and trust.

The Japanese employees in the Occupation, more than 200,000 at the time of its full activity, well understood the nature and purpose of the Occupation and faithfully and uncomplainingly worked with sincere wishes for its success. Moreover, for most Japanese people, the Occupation was the safest place to work. The salaries were comparatively high and were regularly paid even when other offices, public and private, were frequently declaring a moratorium to their employees. I experienced delayed payment just once during my service in the Occupation. "Wait for a few days," they told us. "The money is printing at the Finance Office this minute!"

Outside the limits of the Occupation setup, the place where the greatest number of Japanese people came in direct contact with the Occupation people was the street, now filled with jeeps, U. S. army trucks, and beautiful cars in all shades of luscious colors. Traffic accidents became a serious problem.

The trouble lay in the confusion between the American and the Japanese traffic regulations. The Japanese originally kept to the left and the Occupation people followed the Japanese rule. Some time later, it was ordered that vehicles should keep to the left and pedestrians to the right. But Japanese people, particularly past middle age, found it almost impossible to adapt themselves quickly enough to the new regulation. If some Americans, just out of reflex action, went back once in a while to their homeland motor traffic habit, the Japanese had no right to blame them. But the consequences were serious.

Japanese roads were mostly narrow, crooked and out of repair. They served as children's playgrounds. Neither children nor grown-up pedestrians had sympathy for car-drivers, for to most Japanese, motor-cars were machines not to drive in, but to be driven over. They were such lordly objects that only a very few rich Japanese owned or hired them. Chauffeurs in the employment of wealthy men, as well as taxi-drivers of even rickety, limping 1930 cars, formed a very narrow aristocracy of wage earners in Occupied Japan.

All these factors conspired to produce many traffic accidents. There was no legal procedure for Japanese people to take when hit by Allied cars, even through disregard of the Japanese traffic regulations. This was technically correct in Occupied Japan but it was something which, probably more than anything else, adversely affected the feelings of the masses of the Japanese people. Even in my narrow personal experience, I have known several such cases and have been told that the victim or the bereaved family could appeal to the Japanese government, which, after careful investigation, might pay a compensation, so small, however, that it did not cover the loss of the time, money and labor required in the tedious red-tape procedure.

Cases of plane crashes of the Allied forces were similarly treated. Air traffic became very heavy over the Japanese islands after the commencement of the Korean war, and air accidents, though much rarer than street accidents, did cause incomparably more extensive damage to the people in the hit area.

After complete balancing of the accounts, we may definitely say that the Occupation was a necessary and beneficial expediency for the Japanese people. Under its strong protective hand and ample material assistance, the most effective sanitation and preventive medical measures were carried out. The terrible epidemic conditions expected of a war-devastated nation were almost miraculously prevented. Law and order were maintained until the nation had regained political and economic strength enough to keep itself together, and move on. The rich setup and good pay of the Occupation personnel, which were the perpetual envy of the Japanese people, no doubt contributed much toward keeping up their high morale and personal kindliness, and as a whole the Japanese people entertained a feeling of sincere friendliness and trustfulness toward them.

To the question of how far Japan was democratized under the Occupation, answers will be more varied. But no fair-minded Japanese will hesitate to say that the people learned and gained much. It is too early yet to measure the exact fruits of the Occupation's democratization efforts in Japan, which went on in face of the numerous complex situations and forces weighing on the country and the world. One point, however, is very definite—the liberation of women.

Deepest gratitude is due the Occupation from all Japanese women for giving them complete legal equality with their men, and showing Japanese men good manners toward women. It would have taken ages of hard battling if Japanese women had

had to fight for these rights by themselves. "What would have been our status," Japanese women say thoughtfully to each other, "if our militarists had won the war and continued to rule the country with their brutal force?" This is a candid confession of Japanese women's sincere appreciation of the Occupation. And whatever reaction may set in in the future, the time will never come again when Japanese wives as semi-minors, will be put back under the legal guardianship of their husbands and forced to surrender all their possessions and their labor to the control of the husband and parents-in-law.

There are hot disputes going on now regarding the suggested revision of the new National Constitution in connection with the question of the rearmament of Japan. But even the most reactionary of our men have, as far as I know, never blamed the new Constitution for giving women equal rights with men. We must remember that there are two million more voters among Japanese women today than among their men. Through wise use of their rights our women could control the democratic growth of the country.

26. A Japanese View of the Peace

Seven years ago we Japanese never thought that we would conclude peace with the Allied countries in the manner in which it has been actually carried out. We were told then that the Occupation might last ten, fifteen or even thirty years. The possible duration of the Occupation or any other future prospect

· 239 ·

did not matter much to us when we were completely absorbed in the question of how to eat today. To many of us the future was blank and meaningless.

It seems as if a miraculous leap had been accomplished since those dark days. It is so good to realize that the Occupation, or the long-dragged period of transition between war and peace, has really come to an end and that the Japanese people have regained sovereignty and a future to manage for themselves. Unfortunately, Japan could not conclude peace simultaneously with all the Allied countries, since the Allied nations are divided in opinion. What the country has done and is doing is probably the only way for it to pick its path for peace with the world. The Japanese people, as a whole, are pleased and grateful for the set of peace treaties recently signed and effectuated, and at the same time are anxious to see peaceful diplomatic relations reinstated with the rest of the Allied countries.

Some portions of the Japanese people have shown rather unfriendly attitudes toward the results of the peace conference of San Francisco. They have expressed fear that, as far as Japan is concerned, this treaty will profit only certain classes and not all the people. But we must not forget that these were the most generous terms of peace offered by the Allied countries concerned and that it is up to all the Japanese people to see that they will benefit the entire nation and the entire world. In the delicate world situation in the midst of which the country is tossed about today, the Japanese people must gather peace bit by bit whenever it is offered, and make the best of their chances. Gathering in the cracked fragments of everything good in this troubled world—peace, democracy, international fairness, human tolerance, etc. etc.—with wisdom, discernment and patience, is what our people have got to do after their blind following after vainglorious nationalism.

With the withdrawal of the Occupational control and guardianship, democracy in Japan has now come to be tested in dead earnest. The test will be severe because the Japanese people have plenty of undemocratic weaknesses in themselves, while the conditions of the world are not at all congenial to their free democratic growth.

If by "a modern democracy" is meant a government which respects the basic human rights, and in which the individual wills of all the people are represented by constitutional measures, the Japanese people have still much to work up to. Such ideas as "basic human rights," "expression of individual wills," and "constitutional measures" have not been well understood yet by the masses of our people, who are still governed to considerable extent by traditional sentiments deeply rooted in feudal rule of authority. These advanced political ideas have grown up in the modern Western World, and have been only recently grafted onto the Japanese mentality. They need vigilant care and proper nourishment before they gain new vitality.

It must be remembered that modern democracy is a noble product of the peoples of Western Europe and the United States. Its great humanism and liberalism are certainly two of the loveliest of humanity's achievements. But its high quality is such that it must first grow in the mind of each individual before it can be expressed in social life and political form. Its growth requires time and favorable conditions. The Japanese people as a whole have not had much time yet for democratic evolution, and their poverty and lack of natural resources are not conducive to their liberal, humanistic development.

They face much harder conditions today than the pioneer democratic peoples had to. They must reconcile the difficult relations between their limited material resources and the basic human right of every individual to live a healthy life within their territory. They must, with great racial wisdom, solve their population problem without being beguiled again by the outdated methods of colonial expansion. They cannot just follow any set democratic model from any one nation's past experience.

And indeed, modern democracy is being challenged by the new forces of the world today. The complex interactions of the ideals of Democracy and Communism are apparently absorbing all humanity. The nations of the world are being forced to align themselves roughly in two opposing groups, and Japan finds herself most uncomfortably situated in the middle.

The will of a minor nation is not and can no longer be, respected. A small country, of historical necessity, is subjected to the pressures and tensions of the wills of the major world powers and is thereby bound to crack and divide. It is true that even the people of a big country are divided in thought and opinions, but still they retain a coherent character as a nation. This is no longer possible for a country like Japan, ambiguously situated within the major cleavage zone of the dividing world.

The people of this narrow archipelago, who neither have experienced the glorious material and cultural achievements of

Western capitalistic democracy nor are endowed with enough natural resources to be economically independent of foreign relations, pitifully lack both imagination and self-directing power in the midst of this tense world situation. Naturally, each Japanese is led by his or her immediate personal interests. People of wealth, with cultural and material resources enough to appreciate the comforts and freedoms of American life, enthusiastically call themselves "democratic," while some of the intelligentsia, poverty-stricken and quite out of place in the present state of affairs in Japan, sigh for the status of scholars and artists in the Soviet Russia, so well appreciated, they are told, by the State! To the mentally limited, materially impoverished youth of postwar Japan, the clear-cut, hard-set communist theories and doctrines seem easy to grasp and scientific and rational after the occult spiritual principles of Emperor worship. The unshaken optimism with which the Communists point to the social progress of humanity, is to them attractive and satisfactory in contrast to Western democratic liberalism, which is subtle in thought and often melancholy in temperament.

The opulence of American life, shown through the dazzlingly magnificent Occupation setup, has appeared to the Japanese people entirely marvellous and thrillingly to be envied, but at the same time too foreign to the actual material circumstances of most of them, and therefore too far beyond their aspiration. Any leap at it has ended in miserable tinsel imitation. The heavier-minded, turning away from it, have inevitably faced communism and found the Russian and the Chinese standards of life more friendly and approachable. The generous gifts of food and clothes from American friends have been most sincerely and gratefully appreciated by the direct recipients, but it is quite natural that a poor man should feel shy and uneasy toward his kind and generous rich neighbor and find it rather hard to stand on intimately sympathetic terms with him.

The worst we may fear from Japan's present situation is that the growing antagonism between the two different sets of ideas, now fomenting the minds and destinies of the people, may be easily taken advantage of by men of selfish ambition. It appears that even now, the fallen lovers of power and admirers of force, neither democratically nor communistically principled, but aligning themselves on either side of the dividing line, are watching and waiting for another chance.

The tension of the present world conflict works on the ambiguously situated Japan with such force that unless the country is reinforced with some unified, powerful, external strength, it is sure to crack and be shattered to pieces. For this reason, the Japanese people are glad to have the protection offered by the United States. Only, it is hoped that the people will be wise enough to let the benefit of this defense be shared by the entire nation and not monopolized by any one group. Any unwise use of it will turn the well-intended protection into undue force on the people. Force of any kind, internal or external, well-intended or otherwise, is never conducive to the democratic growth of the Japanese people.

Fears have often been expressed that after the lifting of the Occupational control our once-suppressed fascistic group may regain power. Suspicious minds already discern phenomena that darkly presage the return of some of the old ways. Some people are fearful lest the economic and military assistance kindly offered by the American people is in danger of being used to strengthen the fascist elements in the country. I simply hope that the democratic awakening of the people will be strong enough to counteract and eventually suppress any such tendencies. I have no objection, theoretically speaking, to the rearmament of Japan and the further strengthening of our police power, the two subjects now under heated dispute and severe criticism. But I most urgently hope that our projected army and police force will never be carried away by the same fanatic admiration of brutal force on the part of the leaders, and the same blind obedience on the part of the followers, that caused the Japanese armed forces to commit countless acts of atrocity in the last war. If our army and police go back to the old ways, the entire nation will be easily dragged after them. We must remember that blind following is still a deadly weakness with the Japanese people, and that resort to force in any direction, right or left, is to be more feared than atomic bombing, so far as Japan's future is concerned.

"Peace is here," we Japanese say to each other, feeling as if momentarily balanced on a see-saw. We do not know which way we may turn the next moment or exactly how we shall find ourselves in the world tomorrow. For the present, people living in a big city like Tokyo, with gay boulevards completely rebuilt and far more beautified than the prewar days, get an impression that Japan is rapidly regaining her economic strength and taking to the abundance and colorfulness of American commercialism and free enterprise; that the economic and military support of the United States is sound and secure in this little country on the western fringes of the Pacific.

Just now the country seems geared for the pleasures of rich people only. Comforts and luxuries are displayed everywhere for the moneyed few to buy and enjoy, while the masses are crowded out behind the scenes, together with the discouraging facts of unemployment, inflation, low wages, disabled veterans, war-widows, repatriates, and a general sense of insecurity and discontent.

But this is merely a temporary phenomenon, some people comment. According to them, the Japanese nation, whatever it may appear just now, is after all an Asian race, destined to follow the way led by the Russians and the Chinese, because there is no prospect of Western capitalistic democracy having a chance for healthy, natural growth in Asia.

Others, however, point out that Japan is only on the fringes of Asia and of the world, and that fringes do not count in deciding the main directions of world currents. They will be the more violently tossed up by the centripetal forces of the global revolution, now fearfully forecast. Japan was once a part of the Orient. But as the "golden Jipangu" of Marco Polo, it lured Christopher Columbus westward to his discovery of the New World. The island nation, in complete isolation from the rest of the world, successfully repelled the eastward onset of the European power which overrode the rest of Asia. But it did succumb to the westward expansion of the United States, under whose pressure it eventually opened its doors to modern civilization. Its subsequent growth of feudalistic, militaristic, capital-istic imperialism was finally crushed by the armed forces of the United States, and the country went under the Allied Occupa-tion. Who can vouch that Japan belongs more to Asia than to the Pacific, that final meeting place of the East and the West?

If adaptability is a trait of the Japanese people, that quality is most valuable to them today. Guided by sound brains and realistic humanism, they must gather in from the rushing cur-rents of the world what is truly practicable and beneficial to their national circumstances, and therewith keep their insular position well balanced on the globe. Fortunately there are, it seems to me, a considerable amount of sound-thinking, far-looking, courageous-hearted men and women in this country, who are now staunchly leading and defending the young de-mocracy in Japan. They are our true hope. For to keep the democratic balance of the nation is the only way for Japan to keep peace within the country, and thereby to contribute to the peace of the world.